Designing and Implementing Effective Workshops

Thomas J. Sork, *Editor*

NEW DIRECTIONS FOR CONTINUING EDUCATION

GORDON G. DARKENWALD, ALAN B. KNOX, *Editors-in-Chief*

Number 22, June 1984

Paperback sourcebooks in
The Jossey-Bass Higher Education Series

Jossey-Bass Inc., Publishers
San Francisco • Washington • London

Thomas J. Sork (Ed.).
Designing and Implementing Effective Workshops.
New Directions for Continuing Education, no. 22.
San Francisco: Jossey-Bass, 1984.

New Directions for Continuing Education Series
Gordon G. Darkenwald, Alan B. Knox, *Editors-in-Chief*

New Directions for Continuing Education (publication number
USPS 493-930) quarterly by Jossey-Bass Inc., Publishers.
Second-class postage rates paid at San Francisco, California,
and at additional mailing offices.

Correspondence:
Subscriptions, single-issue orders, change of address notices, undelivered
copies, and other correspondence should be sent to Subscriptions,
Jossey-Bass Inc., Publishers, 433 California Street, San Francisco
California 94104.

Editorial correspondence should be sent to the managing
Editor-in-Chief, Gordon G. Darkenwald, Graduate School
of Education, Rutgers University, 10 Seminary Place,
New Brunswick, New Jersey 08903.

Library of Congress Catalogue Card Number LC 83-82724

International Standard Serial Number ISSN 0195-2242

International Standard Book Number ISBN 87589-992-7

Cover art by Willi Baum

Manufactured in the United States of America

Ordering Information

The paperback sourcebooks listed below are published quarterly and can be ordered either by subscription or single-copy.

Subscriptions cost $35.00 per year for institutions, agencies, and libraries. Individuals can subscribe at the special rate of $25.00 per year *if payment is by personal check.* (Note that the full rate of $35.00 applies if payment is by institutional check, even if the subscription is designated for an individual.) Standing orders are accepted. Subscriptions normally begin with the first of the four sourcebooks in the current publication year of the series. When ordering, please indicate if you prefer your subscription to begin with the first issue of the *coming* year.

Single copies are available at $8.95 when payment accompanies order, and *all single-copy orders under $25.00 must include payment.* (California, New Jersey, New York, and Washington, D.C., residents please include appropriate sales tax.) For billed orders, cost per copy is $8.95 plus postage and handling. (Prices subject to change without notice.)

Bulk orders (ten or more copies) of any individual sourcebook are available at the following discounted prices: 10–49 copies, $8.05 each; 50–100 copies, $7.15 each; over 100 copies, *inquire.* Sales tax and postage and handling charges apply as for single copy orders.

To ensure correct and prompt delivery, all orders must give either the *name of an individual* or an *official purchase order number.* Please submit your order as follows:

Subscriptions: specify series and year subscription is to begin.
Single Copies: specify sourcebook code (such as, CE8) and first two words of title.

Mail orders for United States and Possessions, Latin America, Canada, Japan, Australia, and New Zealand to:
Jossey-Bass Inc., Publishers
433 California Street
San Francisco, California 94104

Mail orders for all other parts of the world to:
Jossey-Bass Limited
28 Banner Street
London EC1Y 8QE

New Directions for Continuing Education Series
Gordon G. Darkenwald, Alan B. Knox, *Editors-in-Chief*

CE1   *Enhancing Proficiencies of Continuing Educators,* Alan B. Knox
CE2   *Programming for Adults Facing Mid-Life Change,* Alan B. Knox
CE3   *Assessing the Impact of Continuing Education,* Alan B. Knox
CE4   *Attracting Able Instructors of Adults,* M. Alan Brown, Harlan G. Copeland
CE5   *Providing Continuing Education by Media and Technology,* Martin N. Chamberlain

CE6 *Teaching Adults Effectively,* Alan B. Knox
CE7 *Assessing Educational Needs of Adults,* Floyd C. Pennington
CE8 *Reaching Hard-to-Reach Adults,* Gordon G. Darkenwald, Gordon A. Larson
CE9 *Strengthening Internal Support for Continuing Education,* James C. Votruba
CE10 *Advising and Counseling Adult Learners,* Frank R. DiSilvestro
CE11 *Continuing Education for Community Leadership,* Harold W. Stubblefield
CE12 *Attracting External Funds for Continuing Education,* John Buskey
CE13 *Leadership Strategies for Meeting New Challenges,* Alan B. Knox
CE14 *Programs for Older Adults,* Morris A. Okun
CE15 *Linking Philosophy and Practice,* Sharan B. Merriam
CE16 *Creative Financing and Budgeting,* Travis Shipp
CE17 *Materials for Teaching Adults: Selection, Development, and Use,* John P. Wilson
CE18 *Strengthening Connections Between Education and Performance,* Stanley M. Grabowski
CE19 *Helping Adults Learn How to Learn,* Robert M. Smith
CE20 *Educational Outreach to Select Adult Populations,* Carol E. Kasworm
CE21 *Meeting the Educational Needs of Young Adults,* Gordon G. Darkenwald, Alan B. Knox

Contents

Editor's Notes   **1**
Thomas J. Sork

Chapter 1. The Workshop as a Unique Instructional Format   **3**
Thomas J. Sork

The label *workshop* is often misused in descriptions of continuing education programs. This chapter clarifies definitions, compares the workshop with other program formats, and discusses its advantages and limitations

Chapter 2. Creating Participatory, Task-Oriented   **11**
Learning Environments
Mary L. Pankowski

Setting the stage for productive instructional encounters requires knowledge of how groups develop, how active participation is achieved and maintained, and how groups can be kept on task.

Chapter 3. Fostering Transfer of Learning to Work Environments   **25**
Robert D. Fox

Workshop participants may have difficulty applying the knowledge and skills gained there in the environments in which they work. This chapter addresses issues of application and transfer and offers suggestions for linking workshop activities with the work environment.

Chapter 4. Planning and Managing Workshops for Results   **39**
Elayne M. Harris

Workshops are typically short-term programs that allow little margin for error. Planning must be thorough, and management must be intensive if intended outcomes are to be achieved.

Chapter 5. Evaluating Workshop Implementation and Outcomes   **55**
Ronald M. Cervero

Determining the outcomes of workshop activities can range from asking participants what they learned to designing complex follow-up studies that assess long-term impact. This chapter describes some evaluation designs and shows how they can be used to assess intended and unintended outcomes.

Chapter 6. Using Technology to Enhance Learning   **69**
John H. Buskey

Many technologies can enhance the learning that takes place in workshops. This chapter reviews these technologies, their advantages, and their disadvantages and illustrates how they can be used in continuing education.

Chapter 7. Postscript and Prologue 85
Thomas J. Sork

This chapter summarizes the ideas presented in this sourcebook, explores future developments that may affect the organization of instruction in continuing education, and provides an annotated bibliography on the planning and implementation of workshops.

Index 93

Editor's Notes

It seems unlikely that any experienced continuing education practitioner can have avoided planning and administering what people refer to as workshops. Short-term, intensive learning formats like the workshop are popular in part because they place few demands on the limited discretionary time of busy adult learners. Acquiring the knowledge and skills needed to design stimulating, interesting, and effective workshops can be a long trial-and-error process. The purpose of this sourcebook is to provide the reader with some perspectives and guidelines on designing and implementing effective workshops. Its chapters have been written by continuing educators, both practitioners and academics, who have experience in the design and delivery of such programs.

Although much has been written about program planning in general and about short-term programs in particular, little literature has focused on the workshop as a unique instructional format. The authors of the chapters in this sourcebook believe that the workshop should be distinguished from other program formats because it can be used to pursue unique goals in a unique fashion.

Chapter One contains a definition of *workshop* that is used consistently throughout the volume. The advantages and the limitations of workshops are identified, and guidelines for selecting this format are presented.

In Chapter Two, Mary L. Pankowski reviews some of the research on group problem solving and offers suggestions for improving participation and task accomplishment in the workshop format.

Participants often come to continuing education programs from a work environment to learn something that they can take back to that environment and use there. In Chapter Three, Robert D. Fox shows how to design workshop activities that can increase the likelihood that the learning outcomes will be transferred to the participant's work environment.

Experienced continuing educators know that administrative oversights can cause programs to fail to meet their objectives. In Chapter Four, Elayne M. Harris discusses the tasks of planning and managing workshops and identifies common pitfalls that the astute administrator will plan to avoid.

Determining the effectiveness of programs is a perennial concern of practitioners. In Chapter Five, Ronald M. Cervero provides a

1

framework for designing workshop evaluations that reveal both the educational outcomes and the links between those outcomes and workshop activities.

Technology, especially microelectronic technology, is developing rapidly. The idea that all instructional resources required for a workshop must be physically present in the room with participants is now an anachronism. In Chapter Six, John H. Buskey provides a comprehensive review of the new technologies and illustrates how they can be used to enrich workshops.

Chapter Seven includes some speculations about the future of the workshop as an instructional format with a brief annotated bibliography for readers interested in learning more about the planning and implementation of effective workshops.

Thomas J. Sork
Editor

Thomas J. Sork, assistant professor of adult education in the Department of Administrative, Adult, and Higher Education at the University of British Columbia, has worked as a continuing education program planner and administrator at Colorado State University, Florida State University, and the University of North Carolina at Greensboro. His current research and writing interests emphasize planning and resource allocation in adult education.

*The workshop has distinctive uses that make it suitable
for pursuing a limited but important category of
learning outcomes.*

The Workshop as a Unique
Instructional Format

Thomas J. Sork

When searching for words to describe the place of workshops in continuing education practice, we may be tempted to use such adjectives as *omnipresent* and *ubiquitous*. Anyone who reads program ads in newspapers or brochures that arrive in the mail may conclude that the workshop format is favored by those who plan continuing education programs. Yet, once the careful reader gets beyond the display copy and reads the program description, he or she soon realizes that many of the events that are represented as workshops are something else entirely. It is perhaps the word itself, or its marketing appeal, that causes planners to prefer it over other, more accurate labels. Or, it may be so widely misused because planners are unaware of the characteristics that differentiate the workshop from other program formats. Indeed, some writers have contributed to the confusion by defining and describing workshops in such broad terms that any short-term program can qualify.

Conceptual clarity can help to improve discussions of workshops. In this chapter, I present a definition of workshop that all the other authors will use. Next, I compare the workshop with other program formats and discuss its particular advantages and limitations. Finally, I propose a general set of guidelines that readers can use to

T. J. Sork (Ed.). *Designing and Implementing Effective Workshops.*
New Directions for Continuing Education, no. 22. San Francisco: Jossey-Bass, June 1984.

decide whether the workshop format is appropriate for the pursuit of a given learning outcome.

Defining Workshops

After reviewing the literature on methods and instructional formats often used in continuing education, I conclude that definitions have become broader and less precise over the years. Recent authors seem not to know of earlier efforts to develop precise, theoretically and practically useful definitions of the workshop format, or they do not see the utility of such definitions. Here are two definitions, each more than twenty years old, that attempt to differentiate the workshop from other instructional formats: "The workshop allows considerable flexibility. Emphasis is on improving individual proficiency and understanding. Theory and practice are often treated concurrently. The learner is encouraged to work out a program of personal study, for which he receives help from other participants and resource people. The learning situations tend to be based on interests and needs identified by the participants themselves (rather than by experts)" (Bergevin and others, 1963, p. 224). "As the word implies, a workshop means work. It is a meeting of people who work together in small groups, usually upon problems which they derive themselves. Complete participation is the keynote of a workshop, because it is expected that changes in people — their ways of doing things — will result. Stage setting in a workshop includes an identification of the problem or problems, exploration, and attempts at solutions with sufficient reference and background material available. An able guide is usually present to bring his experience and previous training to bear upon the problem" (Morgan and others, 1963, p. 61).

Contrast those descriptions with three more recent: "We define *workshop* as a scheduled seminar in some specialized field that has primarily a participatory approach to learning. What we refer to as a *workshop,* others may refer to as a *seminar, course, class, discussion group,* or *laboratory experience"* (Cooper and Heenan, 1980, p. xi). "The main purpose of the workshop is to learn how to do something better or to understand something better. Participants adopt the role of learners. Resource persons have high expertise and behave as instructors. The workshop may include the learning of skills and thus involve much practice" (This, 1979, p. 51). "In this book I am using the word *workshop* to encompass all those learning activities that occur in group settings. A workshop, then, is any group meeting that has adult learning as a *primary* purpose" (Davis, 1974, pp. 4–5).

The images evoked by the first two definitions seem to tell us much more about intent and process than the last three do. Credit is due to all these authors for providing their readers with an image of what they intend to discuss. But, it is disturbing that recent authors fail to acknowledge earlier work that does a much better job of identifying the characteristics that distinguish workshops from other instructional formats. Even if the recent authors disagree with the older definitions, the basic canons of professional scholarship require them to present their case against these definitions and allow readers to decide which definition is more useful.

Because this sourcebook treats the workshop as a unique format, the definition of *workshop* used in its chapters is much more precise than the three just presented, but it is also true to the spirit, if not the letter, of the first two definitions. In this sourcebook, the term *workshop* refers to a relatively short-term, intensive, problem-focused learning experience that actively involves participants in the identification and analysis of problems and in the development and evaluation of solutions. As a temporary educative system, the workshop provides people concerned about a common problem with an opportunity to come together to share their own and others' knowledge and experience and to develop and practice new capabilities under the leadership of a person who can orchestrate the process so that the limited time available is used efficiently and the desired outcomes are achieved.

Related Program Formats

Several other short-term instructional formats are closely related to the workshop, but they should be differentiated from it. The formats most closely related to, and most likely to be confused with, the workshop are the seminar, institute, clinic, and short course.

The seminar is a session or series of sessions in which "a group of experienced people meet with one or more knowledgeable resource persons to discuss a given content area. The participants are expected to be quite knowledgeable, and resource persons expect to learn from them. A great deal of information and experience is exchanged. Often, there is more expertise in the participants than in the resource persons. It is not expected that either problem solving, action, or planning will necessarily result from the meeting" (This, 1979, p. 50).

An institute is a short-term, often residential program that fosters intensive learning on a well-defined topic. "Those who come together in an institute are interested in a specific field. In the institute, new material is presented to add to the knowledge which the participants already have on the subject" (Morgan and others, 1976, p. 66).

Although problem solving can occur during an institute, the primary focus is on the presentation and acquisition of new knowledge under the direction of experts.

The clinic shares several characteristics with workshops. Most often, it is a short-term program that emphasizes diagnosis and treatment of problems that participants bring to the session (Knowles, 1980). However, experts available at the clinic, rather than participants themselves, have primary responsibility for diagnosing problems and prescribing treatment. Thus, although the clinic and the workshop both focus on problem solving, the roles of experts and participants are different in the two formats.

The short course is an abbreviated, more focused version of the class typically found in colleges and universities. Designed to update or deepen the knowledge of those in a particular field, it rarely appeals to a general audience. The expert dominates its sessions, because it focuses on communication and on acquisition of information within a short time.

Although the nuances that distinguish these four instructional formats from the workshop format and from one another may seem slight, a consistent set of definitions could benefit the field of continuing education in several ways. First, communication among practitioners would improve because the words that they use would have the same meaning. As things now stand, workshop planners have no shared image of the program's structure or of the roles that experts and participants will play. Second, the clients whom continuing educators serve would know what kind of learning experience they could expect for their money. Those who registered for a workshop would have very different expectations about the learning experience and about outcomes from those of registrants for a clinic, short course, institute, or other type of program. Third, research focused on the various types of short-term formats might yield cumulative findings that were more generalizable than those now possible with the myriad definitions in use. It is difficult to formulate principles to guide practice if the phenomenon under study is not consistently defined.

Advantages and Limitations of Workshops

Every instructional format used in continuing education has advantages and limitations, which planners should understand. Decisions about format always involve trade-offs. For example, concentrating the learning into one or two days means that more people may be able to attend, but it also means that there is little time for reflection or for integrating new learning with past experiences. So, with a little thought, it is not difficult to identify a limitation that corresponds to each advantage and an advantage that corresponds to each limitation. The advantages and limitations of the workshop format identified in this section also apply to other short-term formats.

Advantages. The workshop format has seven clear advantages. First, due to its short-term nature, many more people can participate. It is much more difficult to arrange one's life to attend a month-long or semester-long program than it is to arrange to attend a one- to three-day workshop. Second, the workshop is very transportable. It can be repeated several times in several locations, because it is relatively easy to schedule both the facilities and the other resources required. This advantage makes it possible to serve clients in geographically isolated areas who may not be able to afford the costs of traveling to a major metropolitan area. Third, workshop participants can apply the results of their problem-solving efforts immediately without having to wait the many weeks that it takes for a longer program to conlude. Interest tends to remain high because the learning is concentrated. Gratification does not have to be delayed. Even though the primary impact of the program may not become apparent until months or years after it concludes, participants can begin to apply their new capabilities immediately. Fourth, the intense nature of the workshop format forces people to interact in novel ways to accomplish a common goal. The personal relationships that emerge among the participants in such an experience can develop into a more or less permanent support system or friendship network that is not likely to develop in lower-intensity program formats. Fifth, the workshop participant is both an emigrant and an immigrant: He or she temporarily leaves one environment or social system and temporarily enters another (Benne and Demorest, 1970). Although a certain amount of environmental baggage always accompanies learners to workshops, removing them from their natural setting for the time of the program isolates them from distractions and day-to-day concerns and enables them to concentrate on the problem at hand. Sixth, well-designed workshops can help participants to refine their problem-solving skills. By observing how others approach problem-solving activities, individuals can identify role models and improve their own capabilities. They can leave the program not only with a solution to an existing or anticipated problem but with increased capabilities to attack future problems. Seventh, from an administrative perspective, the workshop format is attractive because it requires few if any changes in room arrangement or equipment. Although it does require flexible facilities and careful advance planning, there is little need to reorganize the facilities and the equipment once they are in place.

Limitations. The workshop format has six clear limitations:

First, because workshops are intensive learning experiences, fatigue or information overload are always possible. Since there is little opportunity for either rest or temporary withdrawal during a workshop, a participant suffering from fatigue or information overload may fail to benefit from the experience. Intensive learning does not benefit everyone. Individual stamina and ability to sort and process incoming information affect the value of this format for individual learners. A second and related limitation is that the format makes it difficult to take corrective action if an individual learning problem becomes apparent. Because of the pace of most workshops, little can be done to tutor or otherwise assist the learner who has problems keeping up with other participants. This limitation suggests that prospective participants should be made aware of any prerequisite capabilities that they must have if they intend to enroll in the program. Third, those who have led workshops are aware that fatigue can also affect staff. Fourth, once a workshop begins, there is little opportunity to correct problems that arise. Equipment failures, sessions that last longer than expected, meals that are served late, and sessions that begin late are minor inconveniences in longer programs, but in the workshop they become critical events. There is little margin for error in administrative and instructional planning and implementation. Fifth, because time is limited, it is difficult to provide individual feedback to learners. It is much more feasible to have learners evaluate their own work or to have them evaluate one another's work. Feedback is an important facilitator of learning, and it should somehow be designed into the program. Sixth, workshops are participatory learning activities, yet those who attend do not always possess the capabilities required for effective participation. Unless the workshop leader is quite skillful or unless the workshop includes a component that provides training in participation, the group process may become an obstacle to, rather than a means for, attaining workshop objectives.

The experienced planner can doubtless identify other advantages and limitations of the workshop format, especially for particular groups of learners and for particular types of problems. The advantages and limitations enumerated here are presented as a basic list that workshop planners and leaders should consider as they go about the task of designing workshops. Planners who are aware of both advantages and limitations can design a program so as to maximize the former and minimize the latter.

Guidelines for Selecting the Workshop Format

It should be clear from the foregoing that the workshop can indeed be considered a distinctive format for the delivery of continuing education and that it has both advantages and limitations, which planning should take into account. In this section, I will present some guidelines that can be considered when deciding whether to use the workshop format. These guidelines address basic issues. Thus, they are not hard-and-fast rules or formulas for success.

First, the workshop should be used in situations where the learning objectives emphasize problem solving. If the primary objective is acquisition of information, another format would be more suitable. Problem solving requires information, but the workshop emphasizes analysis, evaluation, and application of information, not acquisition and understanding.

Second, the workshop should be used for solving problems that are relatively complex and generalized and that require intensive analysis. Less complex problems of a local nature can often better be solved through the efforts of an individual or a committee. Simple problems or problems with "correct" answers do not require the resources, multiple perspectives, and intense analysis that complex problems require.

Third, workshops should be used in situations where the resources necessary to engage in problem solving are available and where they can be effectively incorporated into workshop activities during a concentrated period of time. Participants will become quite frustrated if they need a resource that is not available to continue or complete their tasks.

Fourth, the workshop should be used only if skilled leadership is available. Orchestrating the events of a workshop requires a unique set of skills, which develops through training and experience. Planners should be sure that would-be workshop leaders can provide evidence that they have acquired the needed skills and that they can apply them with those who will be attending.

Fifth, the workshop should be used only if participants come with, or can be provided with, the group process skills that they need to engage in effective problem solving. Although the skills of the workshop leader can attenuate problems in group maintenance and task accomplishment, it is important for participants to be given major responsibility for maintaining a friendly, supportive, accepting, but task-oriented learning environment.

Sixth, the workshop should be used in situations where it is important to remove participants from their "natural" environment to bring about the desired changes in capabilities. If some characteristic of the environment in which the learner functions retards change, the intense, isolated context that the workshop creates can promote and reinforce the desired changes. Of course, since the workshop context is temporary and since participants will return to their natural environment, the workshop should include activities that suggest ways of over-coming restraining forces that prevent application of new capabilities.

Summary

The workshop can be considered a unique instructional format for continuing education programs. Although it shares some character-istics with other formats, it has features that make it unique and uniquely suited to achieving a particular type of learning outcome. Although it shares some advantages and limitations with other short-term formats, the workshop format possesses a unique set of advantages and limita-tions that those who would use it should understand.

It is arguable that this attempt to distinguish the workshop from other program formats will have an impact on those who prefer to use the term in a more inclusive sense. I have argued that consistent use of a precise definition would have several benefits for continuing educa-tion. Recent writers seem to have ignored early efforts to provide a pre-cise definition, so I write with guarded optimism. Nevertheless, if experienced practitioners and newcomers to the field value the poten-tial benefits of precise definitions, there is hope that the terminological thicket will be cleared and that a way will be opened to better under-standing among practitioners and between practitioners and those whom they serve.

References

Benne, K. D., and Demorest, C. K. "Building the Conference Community." In W. W. Burke and R. Beckhard (Eds.), *Conference Planning*. (2nd ed.) Washington, D.C.: NTL Institute for Applied Behavioral Science, 1970.

Bergevin, P., Morris, D., and Smith, R. M. *Adult Education Procedures: A Handbook of Tested Patterns for Effective Participation*. New York: Seabury Press, 1963.

Cooper, S., and Heenan, C. *Preparing, Designing, and Leading Workshops: A Humanistic Approach*. Boston: CBI, 1980.

Davis, L. N. *Planning, Conducting, and Evaluating Workshops*. Austin, Texas: Learning Concepts, 1974.

Knowles, M. S. *The Modern Practice of Adult Education: From Pedagogy to Andragogy*. (Rev. ed.) Chicago: Association Press/Follett, 1980.

Morgan, B., Holmes, G. E., and Bundy, C. E. *Methods in Adult Education*. (2nd ed.) Danville, Ill.: Interstate Printers, 1963.

Morgan, B., Holmes, G. E., and Bundy, C. E. *Methods in Adult Education*. (3rd ed.) Danville, Ill.: Interstate Printers, 1976.

This, L. E. *The Small Meeting Planner*. (2nd ed.) Houston: Gulf, 1979.

Thomas J. Sork is assistant professor of adult education in the Department of Administrative, Adult, and Higher Education at the University of British Columbia.

Research on group structure and process suggests ways of
enhancing participation and problem solving in workshops.

Creating Participatory, Task-Oriented Learning Environments

Mary L. Pankowski

With Chapter One on the workshop as a unique instructional format as background, this chapter will focus on ways of creating participatory, task-oriented learning environments. It is written mainly from the perspective of the resource person or workshop leader. Chapter Four will deal with results-oriented workshops from the vantage point of workshop planners and managers. Research has shown that a number of factors inhibit or facilitate group interaction and affect both the quality of a group's solutions to problems and the learning that takes place during the problem-solving process. I will discuss those factors in this chapter. They include the nature of the problem, the size and composition of the group, the communication network, motivation, cohesiveness, and leadership. I will also suggest ways in which research findings can be applied to workshop design.

The Nature of the Problem

The relative proficiency of groups and individuals in problem solving depends in part on the characteristics of the problem that is

T. J. Sork (Ed.). *Designing and Implementing Effective Workshops.*
New Directions for Continuing Education, no. 22. San Francisco: Jossey-Bass, June 1984.

addressed. Some problems are so complex that solving them is best accomplished by assigning specialized tasks to different persons. Others demand more information or different points of view than a single person is likely to possess (Kelley and Thibaut, 1969). Still other kinds of problems can best be dealt with by individuals working alone — perhaps because two or more individuals get in each other's way (Thorndike, 1938) or because the solution, once it has occurred to one person, is so obvious that the others accept it immediately (Faust, 1959).

Depending on the amount of information available, problems can be classified as well structured, semistructured, or ill structured (Von Grundy, 1981). For a well-structured problem, all the information needed to close the problem gap is available. Such a problem is typified by its routine, repetitive aspects, and it usually can be solved using standard operating procedures that provide ready-made solutions. For a semistructured problem, there is enough information to define the nature of the problem, but uncertainty about the actual state or the desired state or about how to close the problem gap precludes exclusive use of routine procedures. Typically, a combination of standard operating procedures and creative responses is required to solve this type of problem. An ill-structured problem provides the problem solver with little or no information on the best way of developing a solution. Thus, the ill-structured problem is best dealt with by groups.

Fisher (1974) distinguishes between problems or decisions that require high-quality technical expertise and problems and decisions that require group acceptance and commitment. In his view, the correctness of a solution to a group task cannot be validated by external means. The only criterion for validating a group solution is the group's acceptance of or commitment to the decision that its members have made. Thus, the only way of validating such a decision is by determining whether it achieves group consensus. To ensure the active participation and maximum productivity of workshop participants, the problems being dealt with should be complex and unstructured and require group acceptance of the solutions.

Group Size

To determine the appropriate size for the group to address a given problem, Thelen (1949) suggests the principle of least group size. That is, the group should be large enough that individual members possess all the relevant skills needed to address the problem. However, since opportunities for each member to speak diminish as groups become larger and since larger groups require more control and are generally less friendly, they tend to be less productive (Hare, 1962). In addition, as the size of the group increases, the average number of ideas produced by each member decreases (Gibb, 1951). According to Doyle and Strauss (1976), a problem-solving group should contain no more than fourteen members. These authors report, however, that if the basic elements of the decision have been sorted out ahead of time, the group can include as many as thirty people. These authors examined the relative advantages of different-sized meetings and established some guidelines about what the resource person can hope to accomplish with groups of various sizes. They divided groups into four categories: those with two to seven members, those with seven to fifteen, those with fifteen to thirty members, and those with more than thirty members. At each of these thresholds, the meeting's dynamics seemed to change.

Working with Two to Seven Participants. Working with two to seven participants has at least two advantages: efficiency in dealing with detailed technical and logistical problems and relatively manageable group dynamics. There are two disadvantages: First, only a few points of view can be represented, so the resulting decisions may not have the same quality and impact as those generated by a group of seven to fifteen; second and more important, this number of people may not be sufficient to generate the sheer number of ideas required for creative problem solving.

Working with Seven to Fifteen Participants. Seven to fifteen participants are ideal for the problem-solving and decision-making tasks that are central to the workshop format. Everyone can participate easily, everyone gets to know everyone else's way of thinking, and the group is small enough that informality and spontaneity can be maintained. This range also seems the most conducive to group creativity. There are two disadvantages: Workshop groups of this size are complex enough that they need to be clearly structured, and the resource person is likely to need both a facilitator and a recorder (Doyle and Strauss, 1976). These roles will be discussed in the section on the communication network.

Working with Fifteen to Thirty Participants. It takes an experienced workshop leader to achieve both productive sessions and active involvement of all participants in groups of fifteen to thirty. As the group gets larger, its members feel less responsibility for making it work. Subgroups often take shape, and they can have hidden agendas. The resulting win-lose mentality and the freezing of viewpoints can make collaboration and consensus difficult. As long as collaborative problem solving and active participation are not expected from such meetings and as long as they are used only for information sharing, meetings of fifteen to thirty can serve some useful purposes.

Working with More Than Thirty Participants. Doyle and Strauss (1976) suggest that, in any attempt to involve more than thirty people in problem solving, the resource person will need to divide them into subgroups of less than fifteen. The resource person can help participants to feel that they are part of a larger team by periodically shuffling the membership of the subgroups. Groups based on interest or problem area should contain a representative cross section of participants. The whole group can reassemble for reporting, information sharing, and informal adoption of decisions hammered out in the subgroups.

Large groups are appropriate for lectures, panel discussions, and formal debates but not for workshop task groups. Once the group exceeds thirty, it makes little difference how many people are present. Any kind of participation has to be subject to a clear set of rules. Parliamentary procedures can be useful for this purpose (Doyle and Strauss, 1976).

Maier (1970) points out that the need for face-to-face discussion limits the number of persons who can be involved in a problem-solving group. One possible way around this handicap is to have problem-solving discussions with representatives of groups. This technique requires groups to choose their own representatives with the understanding that they must be willing to accept any decisions that their representatives reach. For the representatives to be effective, they must be delegated sufficient authority that they can act as responsible participants in efforts to reach a decision. In the absence of such authority, the resource person may face a lose-lose situation. With workshop groups of more than thirty, the resource person and the workshop planner must take care to avoid creating unrealistic expectations for group productivity. Ideally, the resource person and the planner will work to create workshop environments that maximize opportunities for face-to-face communication. Thus, fifteen participants is the optimum size for the results-oriented workshop. Together, the resource person and the workshop planner can act to control group size so as to maximize active participation and group task productivity.

Group Composition

Another factor that research has shown to be critical to successful problem solving meetings is the composition of the group itself. Goldman (1965) studied group performance and concluded that it is uniquely affected by the abilities of its individual members. There is substantial research suggesting that homogeneity of individual characteristics among group members promotes member satisfaction (Hollingshead, 1949) but that heterogeneous groups are more successful than homogeneous groups in solving problems (Hoffman, 1959; Hare, 1962; Fisher, 1974). Shaw (1971) reinforces the second point by noting that groups composed of members with diverse abilities perform more effectively than groups composed of individuals having similar abilities.

Haythorn (1953) explored the kinds of individual behavior patterns that facilitate or inhibit group functioning. The behavior traits of cooperativeness, efficiency, and insight were found to be positively related to productivity, although such personality traits as aggressiveness and authoritarianism tended to reduce group effectiveness. These conclusions were supported by Harrison (1965). However, as Krech and others (1962) point out, the qualities of a group's functioning cannot be accounted for wholly by the characteristics of individual members. The particular pattern of individual characteristics within the group must also be taken into consideration. Thus, to the extent possible, the resource person will want to select participants who have the skills needed to solve the problems at hand. To facilitate group effectiveness, the group should be heterogeneous and contain as few dogmatic personalities as possible. If participation cannot be controlled, the resource person should maximize heterogeneity in assignments to smaller task groups.

The Communication Network

Regardless of the characteristics of individual members, the communication network within the group can be changed in ways that increase its productivity. Feedback from receiver to sender increases the accuracy of the messages transmitted through a communication network (Leavitt and Mueller, 1951) so that groups in which communication is maximized are generally more accurate in their judgments. After studying several hundred small groups, Hall (1971) found that the most effective groups were those that tried to get every member involved. This finding reinforces the theory of Collins and Guetzkow (1964), who suggested that effective problem solving in groups can be facilitated by equalizing participation and communication patterns, because it increases the resources available to the group as a whole.

According to Smith (1983), open and voluntary communication in which a free exchange of ideas, opinions, and feelings occurs is the key to collaborative learning. Making sure that messages are both sent and received as intended must become the responsibility of all group members, not just of the leader. Interpersonal communication becomes increasingly open or authentic to the extent that participants come to feel that they can trust one another with their cherished opinions and remain free from attack.

Fisher (1974) states that effective group decision making is highly correlated with the active verbal participation of the group's members. For group decision making to be effective, nearly all members must participate in the interaction process. Active participation does not imply equal participation by all members. Obviously, equal participation is impossible, and it is not desirable. The contributions of some members will always be more valuable than those of others.

Facilitator. Two roles—facilitator and recorder—are important to group dynamics. Both functions promote active participation and enhance group productivity. The good facilitator makes sure that every member has an equal opportunity to be heard and that every member is protected from personal attack. To do this, the facilitator establishes a positive, nonthreatening atmosphere. Doyle and Strauss (1976) feel that one important way of increasing the effectiveness of communication within groups is by appointing a facilitator. The facilitator is a neutral servant of the group who does not evaluate or contribute ideas but who focuses group energy on a common task, suggests alternative methods and procedures, protects individuals and their ideas from attack, and encourages individual members to participate. Doyle and Strauss suggest several facilitation techniques: clearly defining the role of the facilitator as the steward of the group; getting participants to agree on a common problem and process before the workshop begins; "boomeranging" problems back to group members (for example, "That's a good question. Who knows the answer?"); being positive, complimenting the group; avoiding talking too much; supporting the recorder; accepting the inevitability of mistakes; and helping to educate workshop members about group dynamics.

Recorder. The recorder plays an important role in maintaining and enhancing the communication network (Doyle and Strauss, 1976). As the meeting unfolds, the recorder creates a group memory of what participants are saying. The best tools for making a group memory are marking pens and large pieces of paper taped or pinned to the wall. If the process results in information spread over many sheets, the recorder can prepare a summary sheet for the next meeting. Since this role entails so much work, Doyle and Strauss recommend that it be rotated within the group and that those who contribute by performing this valuable service be rewarded.

The group memory becomes a powerful visual tool that helps members to concentrate and focus on what is happening. It also increases the productivity of a workshop by serving as a readily accessible record of what happened after it is over. Group memory helps the group to focus on the task by providing a physical point of reference, it provides an instant record of the session's content and process, and it guards against data overload by providing a short-term memory — we can only juggle about seven pieces of information at one time. Moreover, group memory stores the group's ideas, thereby freeing group members from having to take notes, and it assures that ideas have been recorded and that ideas have been heard by everyone in the group. It helps to prevent endless repetition, it provides a graphic display — a preferred means of presenting visual information — and it facilitates problem solving by retaining information developed in one step for use in a later step. It encourages participation by recording ideas without attributing them to their contributors; it increases the group's sense of accomplishment, because it enables group members to see the work that has been done; and it maintains continuity within a meeting. Finally, it makes it possible to brief latecomers easily, it reduces ambiguity — names, action items, and deadlines are recorded during the sessions to avoid later controversy and confusion about tasks and responsibilities — it is low in cost, and it is easy to use.

Motivation

The effectiveness of a group depends in part on the willingness of its members to work together on solutions to problems. The deleterious effects of low group task motivation on group productivity were documented by Fouriezos and others (1950). These researchers found that the amount of self-oriented behavior — behavior directed not at solution of the group's problem but toward satisfaction of the individual's needs, regardless of its effect of the attainment of the group goal — correlated negatively with measures of group productivity.

Workshop leaders and resource persons often must work both with people who have very little vested interest in solving the problem at hand and who may just be passing time and with people who have too much vested interest and who may therefore have hidden agendas that work against group productivity. According to Hon (1980), a perceived mandate, which makes the outcome of the meeting seem to be important to the superiors of those in attendance, can often be used to motivate participants who have no intrinsic motivation.

Coch and French (1948) found that individual motivation to complete group tasks could be increased by involving the members in deciding on which tasks to accomplish. Thus, the resource person may have to develop goals for the group based on its members' suggestions.

The group must first agree on a task. Only then is there some chance of productivity. But, since the very definition of workshop requires this procedure, it should have an explicit place in the outline of events. Another way in which the workshop leader can enhance motivation is by having the recorder display the results of the meeting on flip chart sheets as they occur. This increases the sense of accomplishment of group members, since they can see a summary of the work that they have done on the walls around them (Doyle and Strauss, 1976).

As Maier (1970) states, the problem situation itself may have a good deal of intrinsic motivation for the group. Nevertheless, the workshop leader and the resource person must consider the degree to which individuals will respond to a challenge. Fear of failure and need for achievement depend on personality factors that influence individual motivation. The stage at which an individual gives up is also a factor in determining a group's success. Intense motivation may even serve as a handicap in that it can generate solution mindedness at the expense of problem mindedness. High motivation can stimulate action that precludes real thinking. Thus, a delicate balance must be struck. As Von Grundy (1981) points out, all persons will not be motivated equally by the same problem situation. Because of differences in individuals' values and needs, their levels of motivation to pursue any given problem situation is likely to vary. A basic guideline is that if closing a problem gap is likely to satisfy the personal need or value of an individual or of significant others (for example, friends, employees, employers), it can be assumed that the individual feels a need to solve the problem.

In summary, the resource person must work with the workshop planner to ensure that at least some participants are able and want to change something and that they know how to go about doing it in a group. The roles of facilitator and recorder can enhance the probability of positive motivation among members.

Cohesiveness

Group effectiveness has also been found to be related to cohesiveness, which is reflected by such things as mutual liking among group members, member satisfaction, and other positive reactions to the group (Shaw, 1971). Results from both field studies and laboratory experiments suggest that highly cohesive groups are more productive if members have accepted the group's task goals. If the task goals have not been accepted, sociability may become the primary goal (Krech and others, 1962).

Numerous research studies indicate that cohesiveness is related to both the quantity and the quality of group interaction. A study by Rawls and others (1969) demonstrates that members who perceive themselves to be proficient in carrying out group functions are more satisfied with the group. Members of highly cohesive groups communicate with one another to a greater extent, and the content of group interactions is positively oriented. Members of highly cohesive groups are cooperative, friendly, and generally behave in ways designed to promote positive group interaction, whereas members of groups in which cohesion is low behave much more independently and show little concern for others in their group.

According to Shaw (1971), the most significant influence of cohesiveness on group action affects group maintenance. The first thing that any group must do is to resolve its internal problems. Indeed, unless it resolves those problems, the group may cease to exist. Therefore, a minimum level of cohesiveness is required for any group to continue to function as a group. To the extent that this minimum requirement is exceeded, Shaw suggests that the degree of cohesiveness will be related to other aspects of group process, such as quality of group product and member satisfaction.

Fisher (1974) reports that as groups raise their level of cohesiveness, it becomes more likely that they will also raise their level of productivity. Conversely, as the group becomes more productive, so does the likelihood that it will become more cohesive. However, Fisher points out that the relationship breaks down at the upper end of the two continua. Extremely cohesive groups are more likely to have moderate to low productivity. Although it may not sink to the level of groups in which cohesion is minimal, it is nowhere nearly as high as it is in groups with moderately high cohesiveness. One explanation for this phenomenon is that some groups may have been together so long that their purpose becomes primarily social. Their productivity suffers from the fact that members enjoy each other's company too much. Thus, the group with the highest productivity is generally the group with moderately high cohesiveness. This is an important consideration for the resource person who works with groups that will be together for a long period of time.

Membership satisfaction increases with group perception of progress toward achieving group goals and of freedom to participate. Perceived freedom to participate, rather than equal participation, should be the goal of a group whose members are happy with their group experience (Maier, 1970). Thus, as the resource person is able to record success in accomplishing group tasks and provide group members with opportunities to participate in group discussion, the group will experience the sense of cohesiveness that is essential to workshop productivity.

Leadership

Many of the concepts just discussed, such as nature of the problem, group size and composition, communication network, and cohesiveness, that affect member participation and group productivity, overlap and complement each other. No factor fits this description better than the concept of leadership. In a way, leadership touches all the other factors and either minimizes or maximizes their impact on group productivity.

Cartwright and Zander (1968) summarized the early research on leadership by stating that the conception of leaders as people who possess certain distinctive traits has proven unsatisfactory. A new view of leadership is emerging that stresses the performance of functions that permit the group to achieve its preferred goal. This point of view has been affirmed by a number of researchers, including Cattell (1951), French (1949), Gibb (1947), Stodgill (1948), and Likert (1959). These theorists point out that the nature of leadership varies from group to group. Situational aspects, such as the nature of the group's goals, the group's composition, the needs of group members, and the expectations placed on the group by its external environment, help to determine which functions will be needed at any given time and which members will perform them (Cartwright and Zander, 1968).

Leadership functions have been classified by numerous social psychologists—for example, Newcomb and others (1965), Krech and others (1962), and Cartwright and Zander (1968)—into two categories: achievement of specific group goals and maintenance or strengthening of the group itself. Thus, the leadership functions that must be performed if a group is to be effective are the task function and the group maintenance function.

The task function involves facilitating and coordinating group efforts to solve problems. According to Newcomb and others (1965, p. 477), for a group to be effective in solving problems, its members must possess certain qualities and have mastered the behaviors related to task achievement: "They are knowledgeable about matters related to the task; they are imaginative, innovative; they are hardheaded, realistic; they are persuasive, convincing in obtaining group consensus; they are good at formulating problems or summarizing discussions; they are skilled in planning, organizing, coordinating; they can be depended on to carry through."

The group maintenance function involves member activities

that help to make the relationships among group members satisfying. Behaviors that are directly facilitative in such ways include the following: "providing warmth, friendliness; conciliating, resolving conflict, relieving tension, providing personal help, counsel, encouragement; showing understanding, tolerance of different points of view; showing fairness, impartiality" (Newcomb and others, 1965, p. 481). Achievement of group goals is facilitated to the extent that its members have the skills to perform both the task and the group maintenance functions.

Although the research shows that any member can perform these functions, specialists sometimes emerge. According to Bales and Slater (1955), studies of problem solving by leaderless groups almost always report a differentiation between a person who presses for task accomplishment and a person who satisfies the socioemotional needs of members. Heincke and Bales (1953) have demonstrated that where such specialization arises, effective group performance depends on the development of appropriate coordination between the specialists.

Group Process Training

Research has indicated that the most productive problem-solving groups are those that effectively carry out the major steps in the process of solving task and socioemotional problems for the group and its individual members. To facilitate that process, training in group process is desirable for group members. If sufficient ability and experience are present, favorable interpersonal relationships will allow the group to achieve its potential (McGrath and Altman, 1966).

Several researchers have indicated that training in group process tends to increase the effectiveness of group problem solving and decision making (Hall, 1971; Pankowski, 1972). Group process training has been defined as an educational strategy in which a small group works together with a trainer over a period of time to explore their own interpersonal group relations (Golembiewski and Blumberg, 1970). In group process training, members establish, with the help of the trainer, a process of inquiry in which they collect and analyze data about their own behaviors simultaneously with the experiences that generate the behaviors. Each individual can learn about his or her own motives, feelings, and strategies in dealing with other persons. As group members acquire new self-insights, they become able to practice new behaviors, and they obtain feedback on the degree to which the new behavior produces the desired impact. Through group process training, group members can develop skills in diagnosing group behavior and in performing the functions needed to move the group toward its desired goal (Bradford and others, 1964).

Although the opportunities to provide group process training are severely limited in most workshop settings, there are many brief, interesting, and useful exercises that can be used to sensitize participants to important dimensions of interpersonal interaction. For specific examples and suggestions on what should be included in such training, the reader can consult Miles (1981), Collins and Guetzkow (1964), Pfeiffer and Jones (1972), and Golembiewski and Blumberg (1970).

Conclusion

The resource person or workshop leader who is aware of what research has shown about the factors that inhibit and promote participatory, task-oriented learning environments can do much to facilitate a successful learning experience for workshop participants. The resource person needs to work with the workshop planner to decide on the size and composition of the workshop group and on the nature of the problem to be dealt with in the workshop format.

Perhaps the most critical item on which the resource person can work with the planner is the structuring of the interactions among participants and between participants and resource people so that the time spent in the workshop can be both enjoyable and productive. Planners and leaders must be sensitive to the factors related to group productivity, such as motivation, communication networks, cohesiveness, and group leadership, and employ techniques to foster the type of environment that encourages the best efforts of motivated, talented, and sensitive adult learners.

References

Bales, R., and Slater, P. "Role Differentiation in Small Decision-Making Groups." In T. Parsons and others (Eds.), *Family, Socialization, and the Interaction Process.* Glencoe, Ill.: Free Press, 1955.

Bradford, L. P., Gibb, J. R., and Benne, K. D. (Eds.). *T-Group Theory and Laboratory Method: Innovation in Reeducation.* New York: Wiley, 1964.

Cartwright, D., and Zander, A. (Eds.). *Group Dynamics: Research and Theory.* New York: Harper & Row, 1968.

Cattell, R. "New Concepts for Measuring Leadership in Terms of Group Syntality." *Human Relations,* 1951, *4,* 161–184.

Coch, L., and French, L. "Overcoming Resistance to Change." *Human Relations,* 1948, *1,* 512–532.

Collins, B., and Guetzkow, H. *A Social Psychology of Group Processes for Decision Making.* New York: Wiley, 1964.

Doyle, M., and Strauss, D. *How to Make Meetings Work.* Chicago: Playboy Press, 1976.

Faust, W. F. "Group Versus Individual Problem Solving." *Journal of Abnormal and Social Psychology,* 1959, *59,* 68–72.

Fisher, B. A. *Small-Group Decision Making.* New York: McGraw-Hill, 1974.

Fouriezos, N., Hutt, M., and Guetzkow, H. "Measurement of Self-Oriented Needs in Discussion Groups." *Journal of Abnormal and Social Psychology,* 1950, *45,* 682–689.

French, R. L. *Morale and Leadership: Human Factors in Undersea Warfare.* Washington: National Research Council, 1949.

Gibb, C. "The Principles and Traits of Leadership." *Journal of Abnormal and Social Psychology,* 1947, *42,* 267–284.

Gibb, C. "The Effects of Group Size and of Threat Reduction upon Creativity in a Problem-Solving Situation." *American Psychologist,* 1951, *6,* 324.

Goldman, M. "A Comparison of Individual and Group Performance for Varying Combinations of Initial Ability." *Journal of Personality and Social Psychology,* 1965, *1,* 210–216.

Golembiewski, R., and Blumberg, A. (Eds.). *Sensitivity Training and the Laboratory Approach.* Itasca, Ill.: Peacock, 1970

Hall, J. "Decisions, Decisions, Decisions." *Psychology Today,* 1971, *5,* 41–54.

Hare, A. *Handbook of Small Group Research.* New York: Free Press of Glencoe, 1962.

Harrison, R. "Impact of the Laboratory on Perceptions of Others by the Experimental Group." In C. Argyris (Ed.), *Interpersonal Competence and Organizational Behavior.* Homewood, Ill.: Irwin, 1965.

Haythorn, W. "The Influence of Individual Members in the Characteristics of Small Groups." *Journal of Abnormal and Social Psychology,* 1953, *58,* 276–284.

Heincke, C., and Bales, R. "Developmental Trends in the Structure of Small Groups." *Sociometry,* 1953, *16,* 7–38.

Hoffman, L. R. "Homogeneity of Member Personality and Its Effect in Group Problem Solving." *Journal of Abnormal and Group Psychology,* 1959, *58,* 27–32.

Hollingshead, A. B. *Elmstown's Youth.* New York: Wiley, 1949.

Hon, D. *Meetings That Matter.* New York: Wiley, 1980.

Kelley, D., and Thibaut, P. "Group Problem Solving." In Lindzey, M. and Aronson, T. (Eds.), *The Handbook of Social Psychology.* Vol. 4. Reading, Mass.: Addison-Wesley, 1969.

Krech, D., Crutchfield, R., and Ballachey, E. *Individual in Society.* New York: McGraw-Hill, 1962.

Leavitt, P., and Mueller, M. "Some Effects of Certain Communication Patterns on Group Performance." *Journal of Abnormal and Social Psychology,* 1951, *46,* 38–50.

Likert, R. *New Patterns of Management.* New York: McGraw-Hill, 1959.

McGrath, J., and Altman, I. *Small-Group Research: A Synthesis and Critique of the Field.* New York: Holt, Rinehart and Winston, 1966.

Maier, N. *Problem Solving and Creativity in Individuals and Groups.* Belmont, Calif.: Brooks/Cole, 1970.

Miles, M. B. *Learning to Work in Groups: A Practical Guide for Members and Trainers.* (2nd ed.) New York: Teachers College Press, 1981.

Newcomb, T., Turner, R., and Converse, P. *Social Psychology.* New York: Holt, Rinehart and Winston, 1965.

Pankowski, M. L. "The Relationship Between Group Process Training and Group Problem Solving." Unpublished doctoral dissertation, Florida State University, 1972.

Pfeiffer, J. W., and Jones, J. E. (Eds.). *The Annual Handbook for Group Facilitators* and *A Handbook of Structured Experiences for Human Relations Training* (both published annually). La Jolla, Calif.: University Associates, 1972.

Rawls, J., Rawls, D., and Frye, R. "Membership Satisfaction as It Is Related to Certain Dimensions of Interaction in a T-Group." *Journal of Social Psychology,* 1969, *78,* 243–248.

Shaw, M. E. *Group Dynamics.* New York: McGraw-Hill, 1971.

Smith, R. M. (Ed.). *Helping Adults Learn How to Learn.* New Directions for Continuing Education, no. 19. San Francisco: Jossey-Bass, 1983.

Stogdill, R. "Personal Factors Associated with Leadership." *Journal of Psychology,* 1948, *25,* 35–71.

Thelen, H. A. "Group Dynamics in Instruction: Principles of Least Group Size." *Scholastic Review,* 1949, *57,* 139–148.

Thorndike, R. L. "The Effect of Discussion upon the Correctness of Group Decisions When the Factor of Majority Influence Is Allowed For." *Journal of Social Psychology,* 1938, *9,* 343–362.

Von Grundy, A. B. *Techniques of Structured Problem Solving.* New York: Van Nostrand Reinhold, 1981.

Mary L. Pankowski is associate professor of adult education in the Department of Educational Leadership and assistant vice-president for academic affairs at Florida State University (Tallahassee). She is also director of the Center for Professional Development and Public Service, which conducted more than 789 continuing education programs in 1983 in which 31,933 individuals took part.

Effective workshops include exercises that demonstrate how new knowledge or skills can be applied in work environments.

Fostering Transfer of Learning to Work Environments

Robert D. Fox

More often than not, when continuing educators want to change competencies and performance of a relatively small group of people in a work setting, they choose the workshop format. As a specialized educational method, the workshop can be considered successful when it promotes change in the ability of an individual or a group to perform in a new way and the learner's application of this new competence within his or her organized work environment. Thus, the workshop is a special strategy for changing individual competencies and work performance.

Assuring that new abilities acquired in a workshop can be applied when the learner returns to the work environment is a challenge. This chapter deals with ensuring that the learner's ability to perform is improved as the workshop planners intended and with obstacles that the learner can encounter when attempting to apply the new learning in the work environment. Case examples from the practice of continuing medical education are used to illustrate how barriers to transfer of learning can be overcome.

Integrating Learning into Individual Performance

The practice of continuing education assumes a cause-and-effect model of change. A teaching-learning transaction is conducted within

T. J. Sork (Ed.). *Designing and Implementing Effective Workshops.*
New Directions for Continuing Education, no. 22. San Francisco: Jossey-Bass, June 1984.

the educational program that causes a change in the abilities of learners to perform in specific ways. This change should in turn lead to new or altered performance in the work environment. This model assumes that change in task performance is possible through change in competencies and that change in competencies is possible through systematic instruction. The success of a workshop designed to foster both change in competence and change in performance depends on the willingness and ability of learners to develop or alter competencies and to apply these competencies to performance in the work environment. In developing educational procedures and resources that can facilitate change in both competence and performance, the continuing educator must attend to problems associated with the characteristics of the work environment and with the willingness and ability of learners to develop or alter competencies and to change their performance.

More than thirty years ago, Lewin (1951) provided a durable framework for understanding the stages of change. Lewin's model can guide continuing educators as they strive to develop workshops that can both facilitate changes in competence and foster application of learning in the work environment. Lewin's model involves three major stages: unfreezing, changing, and refreezing. The first stage, unfreezing, refers to creating a readiness to change within the learner. It focuses on the learner's willingness to change his or her behavior, and it calls upon those involved in the change process to motivate the learner. It recognizes that intentional change can occur when existing patterns of behavior are "disconfirmed," when the learner becomes anxious about the appropriateness of present competence and performance, and when the creation of psychological safety allows the learner to pursue change without serious threat or significant obstacles.

Most often, establishing the willingness to change competence and performance in a way that fosters the application of new learning after the workshop ends requires attention to unfreezing in planning and implementation. To create a willingness to change in the learner, workshop planners and facilitators must examine and understand both the work environment and the targeted competencies well enough to disconfirm the present performance of learners within that context, to create anxiety among the learners about the appropriateness of their present behavior, and to remove or substantially weaken the barriers to development of new competencies and change in performance. Assuming that the new performance is more productive and beneficial to both the organization and the learners, the success with which old ways will be disconfirmed and anxiety about the appropriateness of old behaviors will be increased increases as the discrepancies between present performance and more desirable performance become more obvious. However, it is important to note that while low-level anxiety contributes to effective learning, high anxiety can block learning by reducing the feelings of safety necessary for learners to become willing to change. To create the psychological safety necessary for developing new ways of performing, continuing education planners must understand and overcome social or psychological threats associated with new performance. Accomplishing this goal may require them to investigate the relationships between current and desired performance and the ways in which coworkers and superiors evaluate and reward or punish learners in the work environment.

To create a willingness to change among learners in the workshop, both potential learners and others from the work environment must be involved in development of the workshop's objectives and design. The requirement for in-depth information regarding current status of performance, obstacles to changes in performance, and psychological threats (whether real or imagined) means that those who have a stake in the problem must take part in workshop development and implementation. If clients and other representatives from the work environment are not involved, learners may not be able to transfer their learning to that environment, because there seems to be no relationship between the workshop's objectives and methods and the current activities, problems, and characteristics of the environment.

Case Example. In the College of Medicine, a faculty member of the Department of Pediatrics told the assistant dean for continuing medical education that a continuing medical education program on school health was needed. The faculty member reported that she had participated in several M-Team meetings and that there was a need to improve the working relationship of team members. The M-Team was a multidisciplinary group consisting of classroom teachers, administrators, school nurses, special educators, physicians, and psychologists who reviewed individual pupil's cases to decide on appropriate medical and educational interventions. The assistant dean for continuing medical education asked the faculty member to identify all the individuals who had a stake in the problem, regardless of their role. These people were invited to an initial planning session to explore the nature of the problem. At the initial meeting, they all confessed that they were dissatisfied with M-Team meetings, and each identified specific things that others were doing that created the problems. At a second meeting, the members of this committee began to specify the kinds of information that M-Team members would need to make better decisions about cases, the problems associated with the lack of such information or with inappropriate information, and the obstacles to performing differently in the M-Team environment. By the third meeting, the group had identified a significant number of discrepancies between actual and desired performances and constructed a list of problems that inhibited change among those involved. This information was later used in the actual continuing medical education program to create within learners both a sense of anxiety about current practices and a sense of safety that allowed learners to experiment with new ways of running an M-Team within the workshop setting.

According to Lewin (1951), the second stage in successful planned change is called *changing*. Changing is defined as using new information to develop new responses. It involves a cognitive redefinition through the acquisition of information, whether from a single source or from multiple sources. It also involves practicing the new competence within the workshop environment. Thus, in the successful workshop, learners are given opportunities to understand and observe the performance that is the object of the workshop experience and to practice it until they master it. Such opportunities allow learners to develop competencies and to attempt performance within a psychologically safe environment and without major obstacles to either learning or work performance. By practicing the performance in the protected environment of the workshop, learners are able to modify both competencies and performance free of the fears associated with inappropriate performance in the work place. They also need opportunities to evaluate their performance in a controlled setting that simulates the integration of new competencies and performances into work patterns. It is this last element of workshop design that directly addresses the problems of learning transfer, because it establishes a link between successful performance in the workshop and in the work environment.

Case Example. The planning committee for the school health program decided that the program would contain two kinds of sessions. One kind of session would provide the opportunity to observe the performances associated with a successful and well-conducted M-Team meeting about a specific case. The other kind would provide the opportunity to participate in a simulated M-Team meeting assisted by a workshop leader who could critique the learners' behavior and provide them with information that would allow them to fine-tune it. Moreover, because of the differential amounts of esteem and authority that individual members of the M-Team held in the real world, it was decided that learners would also engage in role playing to allow them to occupy a role outside their normal role. This feature was added to the workshop design because planning committee members had suggested that one obstacle to successful M-Team performance was lack of understanding and experience in a role other than one's own. Committee members believed that role playing would allow learners to obtain valuable information about how they appeared to others on the M-Team in their professional roles. Finally, workshop sessions were organized so that inappropriate uses of status or power could be identified and discouraged by the workshop facilitator. Thus, learners were provided with opportunities to observe an ideal M-Team meeting, to practice the performance based on the competencies that they had learned in another role at a second M-Team meeting, and to practice and receive feedback on their application of competencies learned in the workshop in a simulated M-Team meeting. For example, a physician was able to observe how physicians should conduct themselves in a M-Team meeting, to experience how a nurse feels in an M-Team meeting, and to practice the application of new competencies within the relatively safe environment of a workshop simulation.

Integrating Change into the Work Setting

The third stage in Lewin's (1951) model of change may represent the most substantial problem in the transfer of learning from the workshop to the work setting. This stage, which Lewin termed *refreezing,* refers to the processes by which new behaviors are stabilized and integrated into the ongoing service system where they are to be applied. There are two distinct parts to this stage: First, learners must be able to integrate the new competencies into their personality. Second, learners must be able to integrate these new ways of performing into the significant ongoing social relationships associated with the work environment. Bennis and others (1961) express a related concern when they call for changes both in norms and values at the personal level and in normative structures and role relationships at the organizational level. Nadler and Nadler (1977, p. 231) refer to this critical ingredient of the workshop as *linkage,* the purpose of which is "to have the well-defined activities conducted during the conference be the basis for participant behavior back home after the conference." A central problem in the transfer of learning from the workshop environment to the work setting seems to involve the failure to develop a sense within learners of how to integrate new competencies and performances into not only their personality but also the structure and process that characterize their work environment. Without careful attention to this potential problem at the workshop itself, changes in competence and performance may not be transferred to the work environment.

To describe what can be done to foster the transfer of new competencies and performances to the work environment, it is important to identify the obstacles that can interfere with transfer. An appropriate analogy for the problem faced by continuing educators as they attempt to assure that transfer occurs lies in the problems created by introduction of new technology into an existing organization. Technology, which can be defined simply as a way of doing things, often outdistances organizational processes and structures. Until an organization's structures and processes match its technological potential, it performs at less than a desirable level. Any new technology, whether human or material, requires a certain amount of restructuring of both organizational elements and process.

Many of the performance objectives of continuing education workshops are directed toward making a difference in performance within an organizational context. For example, a new medical procedure must be integrated both into the procedures already used by an individual physician and into the ongoing organizational structures and processes of the hospital in which he or she works. Thus, by examining certain features of organizations, we can identify the areas of organizational life that can obstruct the introduction of new ways of performing. By examining some of these obstructions, we can learn some lessons for the design and conduct of workshops.

Among the features of an organization that can interfere with the adoption of a new technology are its value structure; its formal and informal goal structure; the norms, roles, power and authority hierarchies, and sanctions and rewards of its social organization; and its relationships with other organizations and institutions. In this section, I examine how each of these features can become an obstacle to the transfer of learning and to the development of means for overcoming obstacles to transfer within the workshop design. I will continue to tap the school health program to show how these obstacles may have developed and how they can be overcome.

Values

Values can be defined as "deep-seated feelings and beliefs about given objects or goals in life" (Williamson and others, 1982, p. 251). Values can represent either an obstacle or an aid to the transfer of new competence and performance to the work environment. If it can be demonstrated to learners that the outcomes of new performance clearly help to fulfill not only their own values but also values held by coworkers and the organization in which they work, the chances that the new performance will be transferred increase. However, if the outcomes of the new performance are not known or if their value is not interpreted to learners in terms of the existing values of the work environment, values can impede adoption of new performance.

One important consideration in designing a workshop that fosters the adoption of new performance is the values of learners and their coworkers in the work environment. Although it may require formal investigation to uncover these values, the committee of planners who develop the continuing education workshop can usually identify them if its members represent the diverse value perspectives of those who have a stake in the proposed change (Fox, 1981). The likelihood of developing a program that conflicts with the values of the work setting or of learners decreases when persons who may be affected by changes in performance are actively involved in the planning.

Case Example. In developing the school health program, physicians, nurses, professors, parents, teachers, and school administrators attended the planning meetings. This procedure ensured that the value orientations and the relationship between these orientations and the problems that children have in school would be openly discussed at the planning meetings and that they would be taken into account in the workshop design. As expected, some members tended to emphasize the values associated with education, while others emphasized values associated with child health, and still others stressed values associated with family well-being. As a consequence of the mix of value orientations, some fundamental problems in priorities were identified and resolved. Moreover, the value disagreements uncovered in planning were built into the workshop so as to stimulate the value conflicts that could occur in an M-Team meeting. In fact, specific roles were designed to communicate this conflict to others.

Goals

Organizations, whether formal or informal, have statements to represent their desired future. Whether these statements are consensual and tacit or formally stated and documented, they serve as reference points for the behavior of individuals and groups within the organization (Tuggler, 1978). Etzioni (1964, p. 6) defines goals as "a desired state of affairs which the organization attempts to realize." Modern organizations have many goals, which interact to guide behavior. Some goals are oriented toward the environment, while others are oriented toward the means by which activities should occur within the organization. Lack of consensus about goals creates conflict, while consensus promotes teamwork (Kochan and others, 1976).

Most continuing education workshops attempt to develop competencies that affect performance and thereby affect goals. Consequently, there is great potential for goal conflict between the continuing education program and the organizational environment. When conflict occurs, it can inhibit, if not prevent, any transfer of learning from the workshop to the work environment. Thus, it is worthwhile to seek consistency between the objectives of continuing education activities and the organizational goals of participants. However, especially in multidisciplinary workshops, individual teaching and learning activities can affect organizational goals in different ways and thereby encourage transfer of learning to the work environment in some cases and discourage it in others. It is important for planning to attend to goals as much as it does to values. It is also important for the conflict that the new performance can create with the organization's goals to be simulated within the workshop. This simulation allows learners to assess the potential impact of their new performance and to develop strategies for coping with potential conflicts between program impact and organizational goals.

Case Example. Goal conflict became apparent in the school health program when it was discovered that one of the goals of school systems was to avoid lawsuits or risk of lawsuits when school personnel, especially teachers, dispensed medication. Parents and physicans insisted that medications could and should be dispensed in the classroom if the medicines were properly prescribed and documented and if the parents' permission was obtained. All involved had the overall goal of a healthful and productive learning experience for children. However, other goals differed, in that physicians and parents placed a high priority on timely medication, while school systems had protection from legal repercussions as a primary concern. Attention to this conflict in goals within the school health program planning meetings allowed it to be recognized and built into the workshop exercises. Participants then had an opportunity not only to face the problem but also to attempt to develop solutions in a lifelike environment involving all M-Team members in a simulated case.

Social Organization of the Work Environment

The social organization of the work environment is another potential obstacle to the transfer of new learning. Work environments are made up of formal and informal rules of conduct, power and authority hierarchies, and formal and informal sanctions and rewards for performance. Each of these elements of the social organization of work can conflict with attempts to change work performance. Workshop planners and facilitators must attend to the power of these elements to obstruct the transfer of learning to the work environment.

Both norms and rules can affect the extent to which changes in performance are accepted in the work environment. Norms are informal and often unstated guidelines for social behavior. They can govern who talks to whom, how, and about what; who is responsible for what; and how responsibilities should be carried out. Rules are the correlate to norms within the formal organization. Called standard operating procedures, patient protocols, educational work plans, casework guidelines, or any number of other profession-specific terms, these rules for work are usually stated formally in writing, incorporated into professional training, supported by research evidence, and logically related to the organization's goals. The changes in performance that workshops seek to foster are likely to have an effect on both norms and rules. Planning committees must investigate the potential impact of changes in competence and performance that the workshop fosters on both social norms and formal procedures that govern current work performance. When possible, the workshop design should simulate any conflicts between the new performance and the existing norms and performance rules. Such simulation allows learners to anticipate potential problems in transfer of learning within the safe workshop setting and to develop or understand appropriate strategies for solving these problems. Because workshops are designed to alter or replace a current way of performing, simulation of the process by which the old performance is replaced by the new should be part of the workshop design.

If power is thought of as the ability to cause another to behave in a certain way, then authority must be viewed as legitimate power. Although power often accompanies authority, authority does not always accompany power. To some extent, alterations in power and authority relationships are almost certain to occur when new skills are introduced into the work setting. Pfeffer (1978, p. 20–21) notes that "the greater the uncertainty, the more power can be gathered by the subunit that can reduce uncertainty." Thus, introduction of a new solution to an enduring problem in the work environment is likely to reduce the amount of uncertainty associated with that work and thereby to enhance the power of the individual or individuals who possess the new competence. However, it is rare that power moves easily from one individual to another. Those from the work environment who did not attend the workshop may resist the introduction of a new way of performing that enhances the power or authority of others while reducing their own. Thus, power and authority relationships can be critical obstacles to the transfer of learning from the workshop to the work environment.

To overcome the obstacles presented by existing power and authority hierarchies, workshop planners and facilitators may find that they need to understand the organization of power and authority within the work environment and in many cases to place artificial constraints on workshop participants to simulate the constraints that they may face when attempting to do their work in a new and different way. Once again, by simulating the problem within the workshop and by generating feasible solutions, workshop planners can provide learners with a more complete and realistic experience and enhance the transfer of learning to the work environment.

Sanctions and rewards can also affect the introduction of new competencies and performance. Systems of sanctions and rewards are tied to both power and authority hierarchies and to norms and standard operating procedures. It is entirely possible for a learner to attend a workshop, develop a new competence, and perform it successfully in the workshop environment only to discover on returning to the work environment that the new performance is negatively sanctioned rather than rewarded. Lack of reinforcement can also make the new performance unprofitable for the learner and limit the extent to which the new competencies and performance are applied. Thus, both negative sanctions and lack of reward can erode any changes brought about in the workshop. For these reasons, it is important for workshop planners and facilitators to understand the sanction and reward systems that characterize the learners' work environment and to anticipate any problems that incongruence between rewards and sanctions and the new competencies and performances fostered by the workshop may cause.

Case Example. Because of status differentials and the uneven distribution of power among teachers, nurses, physicians, and parents in the M-Team setting, parents who wished to change the performance of M-Teams or to introduce new ways of conducting the case reviews were at a significant disadvantage. In planning the school health program, there was considerable discussion of the norms governing interaction, the different amounts of power and authority characterizing each of the principal roles on the M-Team, and the impact of sanctions and rewards on parents' need to play a greater role in case review and decision making. Committee members felt that, regardless of their actual roles on M-Teams, the workshop should give learners an opportunity to experience the impact of norms, power and authority hierarchies, and sanctions and rewards on many roles within the

M-Team. Thus, the workshop design included role-taking behavior that allowed participants to assume roles other than those that they occupied in their respective organizations so that they could experience the ways in which norms, power, and sanction and reward systems affected those roles. Particular attention was paid to presenting problems that eliminated the relative powerlessness of parents in the case review process.

Contributing and Supporting Systems as Obstacles to Change

As already noted, to foster transfer of learning, workshop planners and designers must consider the problems associated with bringing about changes in the performance of individuals and with the impact of those changes on the organizational environment. However, a third factor is also important in planning and conducting workshops aimed at changing performance. Individuals perform their work within an immediate environment that I have defined as the organization. Organizations and the individuals within them occupy a place within a larger social environment formed by the contributing and supporting organizations that interact both with the parent organization and with the learners. These contributing and supporting organizations operate in two principal ways: Some organizations provide resources that allow learners and their parent organization to perform. Other organizations receive the output of the work of these individuals and the parent organization. Thus, organizations are linked together interactively and interdependently so that any significant change in one organization can affect its products and services. For example, medical schools are linked to undergraduate premedical programs, since these programs provide the graduates who are trained in the medical curriculum. Later, the graduates of the medical schools have a large impact on hospitals, since the quality of the physicians employed in a given hospital is a function of the quality of training that they receive both in medical school and in undergraduate degree programs. The interaction between the university undergraduate curriculum and hospitals is mediated by the medical schools. Any changes in medical school procedures can affect both the procedures of undergraduate premedical training and the kind and quality of the medicine that is practiced in hospitals. This complex interaction of procedures and practices can be affected by the introduction of a new performance in medical school. Any unwillingness of support systems to accept this new performance can inhibit its adoption in the work environment and thereby obstruct the change process.

Workshop planners and facilitators should develop a clear understanding of the complex interaction of organizations that changes in the performance of individuals who attend the workshop can affect. This is necessarily a broad and difficult task, but it is essential both in planning the content and activities of the workshop and in simulating the variety of actors in organizations who affect or who are affected by the changes that the workshop fosters. A clear understanding of the overall functions of the work environment, of the worker within that environment, and of the procedures and mechanisms by which the individual and the work environment interact within the broader complex of supporting systems is essential in overcoming obstacles to the transfer of learning. If the learner occupies a position that is relatively isolated from this environment, the impact of the new performance on supporting systems may be less dramatic. However, if the learner's primary role is to establish contact between the work environment and other supporting systems, the potential impact of new performance on those systems may be very important.

Case Example. One way of understanding the obstacles to adoption of new performance in the work environment that supporting organizations can create can be seen in the role of the school nurse on the M-Team. School nurses link educational organizations with health care organizations. They are constantly called upon to interpret educational practice to health professionals and health practices to education professionals. It was obvious to the workshop planning committee that any changes by the school nurse in the performance of her duties could be obstructed by the attitude toward that change of either the medical community or the education community. Thus, in designing workshop activities for school nurses, it was important to identify and simulate the problems associated with altering the procedures by which medication was handled in the school system. In fact, the requirement that the school nurse should be responsible created a complex dilemma which was dramatically simulated within the workshop experience.

Although this chapter has emphasized what can be done during planning and implementation to ensure transfer of learning to the work environment, follow-up can also encourage mutual adaptation of the new performance and the work setting. Nadler and Nadler (1977) recommend that workshop planners and facilitators use a delayed evaluation procedure. By delaying evaluation until learners have had an opportunity to attempt the new performance in the work environment and to encounter difficulties in transferring their learning, workshop planners and facilitators can identify unanticipated problems. Identification of such problems can help them to improve future workshops, tailor follow-up sessions to the needs of past workshop participants, and attend to the needs of individual learners as they attempt to transfer learning to the work setting. For example, delayed evaluation can reveal that superiors within the organization do not understand the relationship between the new performance and the organization's goals. Identifying the problems soon after the workshop allows program committee members and workshop facilitators to contact superiors directly and explain the relationship or to provide learners with additional written material and consultation that they can communicate to their superiors.

Follow-up activities are important because they recognize the enduring responsibility of workshop planners and facilitators to the effect of learning not only on the learner but also on the work setting. Ideally, problems will not arise, because those who have a stake in the learner's performance have been involved in program development and because potential problems have been simulated in the workshop environment. However, follow-up also gives planners and facilitators an opportunity to follow through on their attempts to ensure change in learners' competence and performance.

Summary

This chapter has identified several methods for overcoming obstacles to the transfer of learning to the work setting. First, workshop planners and facilitators should investigate the value orientation, the goal structure, and the power and authority relationships within the learner's work setting and its interaction with other organizations. With adequate, representative participation and planning and with attention to the features of the work environment just enumerated, it is possible to design a workshop experience that at best has the support of the work environment before it is implemented and that at least addresses potential problems in and limitations on the transfer of learning to the work setting.

Second, problems that can block the transfer of learning to the work environment should be simulated as part of the workshop's formal activities. In particular, workshop planners and facilitators should ensure that the design allows for the simulation of problems created by conflicts between new competencies and performance and organizational values, goal and authority structures, norms and standard operating procedures, sanctions and rewards, and interactions with other contributing or supporting organizations. Simulation is a powerful tool for isolating the learner's first frustrating and confusing encounter with conflicts raised by attempts to introduce new or altered performance into the work environment. Role playing allows learners to experience and develop strategies for overcoming the conflicts inherent in change. Finally, it is important to follow up on learners after the workshop to determine the value of workshop experiences in promoting change in competence and performance and the obstacles that learners have encountered in introducing new performance into the work setting. Follow-up after the workshop complements the concern for the work setting in workshop planning and implementation advocated here.

References

Bennis, W., Benne, K., and Chin, R. *The Planning of Change.* New York: Holt, Rinehart and Winston, 1961.

Etzioni, A. *Modern Organizations.* Englewood Cliffs, N.J.: Prentice-Hall, 1964.

Fox, R. D. "Learner Involvement in Continuing Professional Education: Issues and Suggestions from the Literature." *Lifelong Learning: The Adult Years,* 1981, *5* (4), 22-26.

Kochan, T. A., Cummings, L. L., and Huber, G. P. "Operationalizing the Concepts of Goals and Goal Incompatibility in Organizational Behavior Research." *Human Relations,* 1976, *29,* 527-544.

Lewin, K. *Field Theory in Social Science.* New York: Harper & Row, 1951.

Nadler, L., and Nadler, Z. *The Conference Book.* Houston: Gulf, 1977.

Pfeffer, J. *Organizational Design.* Arlington Heights, Ill.: AHM, 1978.

Tuggler, F. *Organizational Processes.* Arlington Heights, Ill.: AHM, 1978.

Williamson, R. C., Swingle, P. G., and Sargent, S. S. *Social Psychology.* Itasca, Ill.: Peacock, 1982.

Robert D. Fox is assistant professor and director of research in the Department of Continuing Medical Education and Family Practice at the Quillen-Dishner College of Medicine, East Tennessee State University (Johnson City). His current research emphasizes application of adult education perspectives to physicians as adult learners.

Applying the tools of planning and management while avoiding their pitfalls will increase the likelihood that a workshop will produce the desired results.

Planning and Managing Workshops for Results

Elayne M. Harris

Although the goals of individual workshops can vary, they all share a common mission — maximum results, that is, maximum learning. This mission is more than an attractive slogan. It can and should be the overriding criterion when making decisions in planning and managing workshops. The managerial process is often undervalued in workshop delivery. The emphasis is usually placed on the instructional process. Yet, any experienced manager of continuing education programs knows that the goal of producing maximum learning can be thwarted as easily by poor workshop management as it can by poor instruction. This chapter has three purposes: to describe a planning model that can be used to guide decision making, to identify some of the tools commonly used by those who plan and manage workshops, and to explain some of the pitfalls that can be encountered in planning and managing workshops and provide tips on how to avoid them.

The Workshop Planning Model

Workshop planning involves anticipatory decision making. It is a special form of decision making, because it requires the planner to

T. J. Sork (Ed.). *Designing and Implementing Effective Workshops.*
New Directions for Continuing Education, no. 22. San Francisco: Jossey-Bass, June 1984.

base specifications for an educational program on very limited information. Uncertainty is high at the beginning of planning, because both the goals of the workshop and the means that will be used to achieve them have yet to be determined. As planning progresses and as decisions are made, the uncertainty is gradually reduced, because the goals and the means of achieving them are clarified. Unfortunately, complete certainty is never possible, because unknown variables can always affect how the plan is implemented. Using a planning model helps to identify and organize the decision points that are critical for producing an effective program.

Buskey and Sork (1982) have described and evaluated ninety program planning models found in the literature. Many of these models can be applied to workshop design. The authors classify them according to planning context, level of program emphasized, and client system orientation, and they evaluate them for the sophistication necessary for effective use, the extent to which they have an explicit theoretical framework, and their degree of comprehensiveness. The analysis conducted by Buskey and Sork can be helpful to those who must select or construct a planning model for use in designing workshops.

In this chapter, I propose a model that is essentially normative; that is, it describes how planning should be done, not how it is done. This model is general enough to encompass most continuing education contexts, and it should be useful to both beginning and experienced practitioners. It has nine steps: determining financing or budget, conducting needs assessment, selecting resource persons, developing the learning design, selecting aids to support that design, selecting a location, marketing the workshop, conducting the workshop, and evaluating the workshops.

The model is based on seven assumptions: First, the person who plans and manages the workshops is different from the person who leads the workshop. For convenience, I refer to the first person as the *planner* and to the second as the *resource person*. Second, the planner and the resource person must have a clear understanding of their respective roles and of their interdependence in creating a successful workshop. In this model, the planner is responsible for initiating and successfully completing all the program planning steps. Indeed, the planner has responsibility for ensuring that everyone involved in the planning process understands his or her role. Therefore, the planner must also manage the involvement of the resource person. Third, the linear arrangement in which the model is presented is for discussion and analysis only and does not necessarily reflect the order of planning tasks. Planning can begin with the sudden availability of a resource person which thereby eliminates the third step entirely. Similarly, a location for the workshop can be selected (step six) before the workshop design is developed (step four). It is even possible to create a design (step four) before a resource person is selected (step three). Fourth, one step does not have to be completed before another can be started. Thus, work can proceed concurrently on several steps. Fifth, each step is not necessarily discrete. Some blur and run into others. For example, learning design overlaps with selection of learning aids, while the physical space available for a particular workshop can have implications for the learning design or even for the appropriate resource person. The astute planner will be aware of the interrelationships of steps and understand the impact that each decision has on prior and subsequent decisions. Sixth, all the tasks specified by the model must be accomplished. The planner's job is to assure that all necessary tasks are completed, although he or she can delegate the tasks to others. Seventh, it is common that one or more steps have imperatives that arise from the planning context. A staff development planner who is designing an in-house workshop may have to rely on managers to market the program. A university continuing educator may have to use a faculty person whom a dean selects as a workshop resource person. Thus, in some settings, there are few or no alternatives. The planner must decide whether to accept the constraint and continue or to reject the imperative and disengage from planning.

The Planning Timetable

A second tool for workshop management, the formal planning timetable, complements the workshop planning model. The workshop planner needs four kinds of information to construct this tool: a list of the tasks that must be accomplished before, during, and after the workshop; the amount of time needed to accomplish each task; the staff and other resources needed to accomplish each task; and the appropriate sequence for these tasks.

Several techniques have been developed for combining various elements of this information and presenting it in graphic form. One such technique is the Gantt chart—a horizontal bar graph indicating activity, duration of activity, and dates for completion. A more sophisticated version, the Critical Path Method (CPM), is particularly appropriate for complex planning situations. In the CPM, every activity required for project completion is identified, arranged in sequence, and assigned a minimum time and a dollar cost needed for completion. Diagramming of this information produces a sequential network called the *critical path* that reveals the minimum amount of time needed to complete the project. Other related techniques for establishing a time-table and for sequencing tasks are the Program Evaluation and Review Technique (PERT) and the Planning-Programming-Budgeting System (PPBS). Strother and Klus (1982) describe these techniques.

Integrating the Time Line and Workshop Planning Model

In managing workshops, planners can marry these two tools. Since the steps in the planning model are already a rough outline of major management activities, the program planning model gives continuing educators a head start in developing a critical path for work-shop management. Continuing educators then can continue to apply the CPM and assign specific dates so that each day's tasks or each week's activities are clear. As circumstances dictate, planners can produce a critical path and base workshop dates on the network's length, or they can work backwards from dates suggested for a particular work-shop to determine the feasibility of planning the process to meet those dates.

The CPM is not at all complex. Consciously or unconsciously, people use a simplified version of it in their everyday life. Getting to work on time and planning a dinner party require us to consider the same components as those of the CPM. However, combining the pro-gram planning model and the CPM requires some investment of time. One project with which the author was involved took five months with the first month spent in developing the critical path.

Continuing educators who have planned and managed many workshops have an intuitive sense of the pacing of tasks that leads up to a workshop. However, the CPM can help even the most experienced practitioner to remember the hundreds of small tasks that must come together at the time of the workshop. It eliminates the nagging feeling of uncertainty that neophyte planners often experience, and it is a quick reference during those all too frequent days when the press of a heavy workload does not allow for clear, organized thought. Once the critical path has been constructed, it can be used to explain the amount of work involved and the attendant costs to sponsors, superiors, coop-erating agencies, and clients.

Influence of Format on Time Line. The most critical planning decision concerns the total time that must be allowed for workshop planning and management. Generalizations are hazardous, since indi-vidual circumstances vary so widely within the field of continuing edu-cation, but if we consider a workshop that addresses a topic and a target group that are unfamiliar to the planner and that requires marketing by means of a brochure to be mailed in a mid-sized city, a six-month planning time line is not unusual. Of course, the availability of staff is a major variable that can lengthen or shorten the time line.

One distinguishing characteristic of workshops is that they are short-term learning events, sometimes lasting no more than an evening or a half day and rarely exceeding a week. Two understandings that arise from a compressed program format are pertinent to the development of a critical path for workshop management. First, the short-term nature of the event itself does not mean that it takes less time to plan than a longer program. If anything, it takes more time, because planners must be sure that nothing has been overlooked. Second, the details of conducting the event itself, from greeting participants to closing the workshop, must be meticulously planned and reviewed. The reason for both is the same: Workshops compress so much activity into such a short time that there is little or no margin for error.

Requirements for precision in planning and management can be inversely related to the length of the program. For example, booking a location for a one-day workshop involves the same amount of time as booking a location for a semester-long course consisting of twelve evening classes. However, if the location for the twelve-week course turns out to be unsuitable for any reason, the planner has a week's time in which to find a better site and eleven other occasions on which to erase the memory of the original location. In contrast, if the location for the one-day workshop proves unsuitable, the planner who can find a suitable space immediately will be unusually lucky. Moreover, even if he or she does, any change in the site of a program that lasts twelve hours or less creates a disturbance that can have a continuing negative effect on workshop participants. In either case and regardless of how good-natured people are about the inconvenience caused by the move, the participants experience the workshop as one that had a problem. The planner's good intentions cannot change that. By adding time for extra thoroughness and checking to the workshop's critical path network, the planner can reduce the adverse effects of unanticipated problems.

Without a doubt, the biggest trap that awaits the unwary in deciding on a planning time line lies in underestimating the length of time necessary to plan and manage all the workshop's activities. The explicit critical path network developed as a week-to-week guide for the planner may be the document that is most useful in convincing others that the planner is undertaking responsible and professional planning.

Cautions When Using the CPM. The existence of a workshop planning model and the development of a time line create a danger that continuing educators will believe that these tools will always produce success. However, this belief should dissipate when we examine the three sources of information needed to combine the planning model with the CPM to produce a working document for workshop management. These three sources are the research literature on adult education, consultation with others who have managed similar workshops, and considered judgments that planners will have to make about the particular workshop. The third source is important, because it reminds continuing educators, who strive to eliminate as much uncertainty as possible, that workshop management entails many judgment calls. It is often in this arena that opinions are mistaken for facts, that judgements are not realized, and that causes for unsuccessful workshops can develop.

To illustrate that a time line integrated into a workshop planning model does not necessarily produce consistent success, consider step seven, marketing the workshop. One common marketing strategy for workshops is the mailed brochure. In applying the CPM, the planner must decide how long before the workshop takes place to mail the brochure. Here are some of the factors to be weighed in making this decision — which is potentially only one of hundreds: Which class of mail can the budget afford? How long does each class of mail take for delivery? Are Postal Service estimates for delivery time reliable? How many of the potential participants are familiar with the sponsoring institution? Those who are not will need some time to find out about it. How much time should be allocated for this? Is the workshop during regular working hours? Most people have to obtain permission from their employers to attend a professional developing event during working hours. How does that consideration affect the time that elapses between the mailing of the brochure and the final date for registration? How much does the workshop cost? Will participants pay for the event themselves, or will their employers subsidize their attendance? If they have to apply for employer support, how much time should the planner allow? What is the life-style of intended participants? How far in advance do individuals in this group schedule their personal and professional activities? What other professional development activities may be competing for the intended participants' professional development budget? How early must the brochure be mailed so that it reaches intended participants before information about other competing events? Finally, how enticing is the workshop? This can depend on many factors — the drawing power of the resource person, the uniqueness and timeliness of the workshop's topic and the educational need that the workshop addresses, the registration fee, the effectiveness of the brochure, and so on. Will it be enticing enough that life-styles and competing events will not affect decisions to participate? The answers to these questions depend on past experience and informed opinion — and in many cases on rough estimates and guesses. That makes the design only as good as the decisions, whether the decisions are based on fact or on opinion.

Planner's Role in Climate Setting

Since workshops are short-term by definition, every minute counts toward results. Therefore, when working in the tight timeframe imposed by a workshop, the less time the workshop leader has to budget for climate setting, the more time can be allotted for learning. While climate setting is commonly considered to be the responsibility of the resource person, the planner can also play a supportive role. If the planner has managed the planning and administrative process so that participants begin the workshop as free as possible from distractions, frustrations, or questions, the time required by the resource person for climate setting will be shortened.

The planning and administrative processes that are visible to workshop participants can subtly but significantly influence the desired mind-set. Quality of on-site arrangements, advance information, concern for learner needs, friendliness, and personal attention can do much to create a climate that is conducive to learning. The converse is also true. Thus, it behooves planners to approach each task in the workshop planning model with the understanding that how well it is executed will affect climate setting and therefore learning outcomes.

Employing the Workshop Planning Model

The remainder of this chapter provides an overview of the components in the workshop planning model and suggestions for ensuring that the program's intended outcomes are attained. It does not attempt to be a how-to guide for planners; instead, it highlights key information, pitfalls for the unwary, and considerations born of experience gained in planning hundreds of workshops.

Determining Financing or Budget. Unless the planner is given a blank check to cover workshop expenses, the cost of the following items must be taken into consideration: the resource person's time; the workshop site; workshop materials, including books, papers, instructional media, and other learning aids; marketing; participants' meals, coffee breaks, and possibly accommodation, transportation, and hospitality; staff time for planners and other professional or support services persons, such as graphic artists, secretaries, and registration personnel; and needs assessment and evaluation.

Pitfalls in Budgeting. There are two dangers in budgeting: underestimation of the actual costs of items and failure to anticipate all the items needed. The cost of items that seem minor — such as coffee — can surprise even experienced planners.

One common problem area is in reaching agreement with workshop leaders about their fees. Planners should be certain to clarify whether the fee includes planning time and the number of contact hours that it covers. In North America, continuing educators should be alert to the differing value of American and Canadian dollars when discussing fees.

In general, planners should consider it appropriate to negotiate fees with resource persons, treating the figure that they name as their usual per diem as an opening position. Some factors for planners to keep in mind when negotiating fees are the publicity that a resource person will receive from the planner's marketing efforts, the opportunity for contracts from workshop participants who are favorably impressed, the financial circumstances of intended registrants, the credibility of the resource person and the drawing power of his or her reputation, the size of the market for a particular subject area, the prestige factor and the enhancement of reputation that working for certain agencies can bring to the resource person, and the availability of other resource persons for the particular workshop. The publicity factor alone was reason enough for one resource person with whom I dealt to accept a two-thirds reduction in the person's normal fee. Of course, in some circumstances, people who can command substantial fees for their involvement give their services voluntarily or for an honorarium. A quite useful resource for readers interested in exploring this topic is the sourcebook edited by Shipp (1982).

Conducting Needs Assessment. Needs assessment is a process, not just a data-gathering technique. Probably the most misunderstood of all the steps in the planning process, it shares the distinction with evaluation of giving program planners more feelings of guilt about their professionalism than anything else. The primary reason for undertaking a needs assessment is to collect enough data about the learning needs of a particular group that the program planner and the resource person can eliminate as much guesswork as possible in planning workshop goals, objectives, and design. A second reason for conducting a needs assessment is to provide a basis for persuasion. There are many occasions on which concrete information produced by a needs assessment can satisfy a funding agency, a boss, or even the learners themselves.

One important by-product of needs assessment is the marketing information that it yields. A needs assessment that gathers data from the learners themselves is an effective and appropriate way of raising awareness about gaps in knowledge or skill, and it can alert these learners to an upcoming event that will address their need. This function of needs assessment can be reinforced if learners receive information about the findings of the completed survey.

Pitfalls in Needs Assessment. The unwary face some pitfalls in needs assessment. Poorly conceived needs assessments can fail to yield useful planning information. In fact, they can produce misinformation that sends the planner off on unproductive and expensive safaris into the trivial or the irrelevant. It is important to realize that acknowledgment of need is not a commitment to attend a program that addresses that need. Another very real pitfall is that people are not always accurate in diagnosing their own needs. For example, in a survey of training needs in companies supplying the oil industry, managers reported little need. However, the survey was underwritten by oil companies. Would managers hungry for contracts with oil companies do anything but present themselves as confident, capable, and ready to provide excellent services to people who might have control over their future business? Even if responses are anonymous, people tend to give socially desirable answers. Other pitfalls of needs assessment and suggestions for avoiding them can be found in Pennington (1980) and Strother and Klus (1982).

Selection of Resource Person. Selecting a resource person requires the planner to match the workshop participants with the workshop leader. The minimum requirements for success are that the resource person must have credibility in the subject matter, an understanding of the teaching and facilitating behaviors required by the workshop format, a personal style that indicates respect for and knowledge about adult learners and that allows learners rapidly to become engaged in the learning process, and an enthusiasm for the subject matter and for helping others to learn about it. Without these four prerequisites, the success of the workshop is uncertain.

Pitfalls in Selecting Resource Persons. The biggest pitfall in selecting a resource person lies in choosing a person who has credentials in the subject matter but whose skills are not adaptable to the workshop format or who treats participants in ways that are inconsistent with their expectations.

One successful strategy for choosing resource persons has three components. First, a check of formal qualifications is made. This can be accomplished by requesting a resume, checking on publications, and validating self-reports of other accomplishments. Although potential resource people rarely falsify a resume, resumes are written to create favorable impressions, and they need to be read with that reality in mind. Next, personal contact with the resource person is made — by a face-to-face meeting, a telephone conversation, or correspondence, in descending order of desirability. How the potential resource person presents himself or herself, whether the planner feels comfortable with the transaction, and the appropriateness with which the potential resource person responds to inquiries and comments are all factors for the planner to consider. The personal contact is in reality an interview, and resource persons who conduct themselves appropriately are good prospects for workshop leaders. Third, information about the potential resource person can be sought from respected others. Such information is particularly important to planners who know little about the workshop's subject matter. For experienced planners, the third step is a kind of insurance and an opportunity to test their judgment against that of others.

Developing the Learning Design. The planner generally sets the overall goals of the workshop and sometimes consults with the resource person to develop specific learning objectives. Similarly, the planner and the resource person can act as a team to develop the workshop design, although more commonly this task is undertaken by the resource person alone. Planners must assume responsibility for approving the design, at least to the extent of assuring that the resource person has understood the nature of the workshop format and developed a design that is in keeping with it. It is prudent for planners to ask for a detailed workshop plan far enough in advance that adjustments or major changes can be made if required. Chapters Two, Three, and Six of this sourcebook provide useful suggestions and principles to follow when designing workshops.

Pitfalls in Developing the Learning Design. The most common danger in developing the learning design lies in mistaking an agenda or subject outline for a workshop design. Planners should insist on knowing the specific activities, techniques, devices, and exercises that will be used to meet the objectives that have been agreed on. This is particularly important when the resource person is unaccustomed to the workshop format. The planner should be aware that any shortcomings in the workshop's design will be laid at the planner's door, since he or she is responsible for selecting the resource person.

By definition, workshops are short, and there are few subjects that can be exhausted in the workshop format. Workshop designs often err in crowding too much content into the time available at the expense of both problem solving and learner participation. Resource people sometimes do this as a way of establishing their subject expertise. Generally speaking, it is better to concentrate on three or four key learning objectives than it is to deal superficially with a great deal of material. Those involved in the design of workshops must develop the skill to choose topics that can be handled satisfactorily in the short time-frame of the workshop format. Since workshops focus on problem solving, devoting too much time to the presentation of content reduces participant involvement, and it can also reduce the likelihood of transfer. Workshop plans that feature variety, that involve participants actively, that give participants opportunities to apply new content or information, and that provide them with feedback are hallmarks of effective design.

Selecting Aids to Support the Learning Design. The instructional aids required for the program should be evident from the workshop design. It is the planner's responsibility to acquaint resource persons with the aids that can be made available and with the upper limits imposed by budget on the number and type of aids used. The number and type of aids can be decided on jointly by the planner and the resource person, as can responsibilities for preparation of materials, booking of media and equipment, and other tasks related to this step of planning.

Pitfalls in Selecting Aids. The selection of aids is too often based on the wrong criteria. Selection should be based first on the degree to which the aid will foster the workshop's objectives. After that criterion has been satisfied, other criteria can be used to sort through the available alternatives. These criteria can include cost, availability, the resource person's experience and skill in using the aid, anticipated learner acceptance of the aid, reliability of the technology, readability of materials, and so on. In addition to Chapter Six of this sourcebook, Wilson (1983) provides useful information on the selection and development of instructional aids.

Selecting a Location. The time-intense dynamics and special nature of the workshop format legitimize elevation of this function to a discrete step in the workshop planning model. The ideal room for a workshop is spacious, carpeted, well ventilated, and versatile, and it has natural lighting, good acoustics, movable tables, and comfortable chairs. The workshop design and the learning aids used to execute it often help the planner to select an appropriate location. Experienced planners consult resource people about the design before booking a location.

Other considerations in choosing a location are convenience for participants, ease in locating the selected site, and parking. The site should be removed from the natural work environment of the participants so that they will not be tempted to pick up messages, drop in for "brief" meetings, or check the mail. In most cases, telephones should be adjacent to, but not within, the workshop meeting area so that participants can receive and respond to important messages. Advance information should clearly indicate the procedure to follow if someone wishes to get in touch with a workshop participant during the program.

Pitfalls in Selecting a Location. Planners who do not personally inspect the selected location for a workshop take an unnecessary risk. Planners should inspect even sites that they have used before — as close to the date of the workshop as possible but still in time to make other arrangements if necessary. Such inspection might well reveal that the room which had been ideal for a previous program now has problems. Curtains which are necessary when films are to be screened can be removed for cleaning, and furnishings that are suitable for a class do not always meet the demands of a workshop. The planner should be certain, too, that the facility is not scheduled for another event immediately before or after the workshop. Tight scheduling can disrupt the beginning or end of the workshop and make it more difficult to achieve program objectives.

Marketing the Workshop. The first management decisions about marketing the workshop rest on a combination of judgments about workshop participants and a knowledge of marketing as it applies to continuing education. There are three critical decisions: the choice of publicity and advertising approaches, the setting of appropriate lead time, and the organization of people and resources to produce an effective, efficient, and timely marketing strategy.

The first set of decisions concerns the nature of the promotion that will bring in the desired number and type of workshop participants. The use of free promotion — public service announcements, notices in newsletters, media coverage, announcements during professional association meetings — should be limited only by the available time. Vehicles for paid promotion — advertising — include posters, brochures, relevant journals and newspapers, and radio or television commercials. The most frequently used and cost-effective marketing tool is likely to be a brochure sent to a carefully compiled list of prospective participants.

The second critical set of decisions involves the length of time that elapses between the date on which potential participants receive information about the workshop and the date on which the workshop begins. A minimum of six weeks is recommended. The length of time can be increased if the workshop is particularly expensive, if absence from work is required, if participants need to make special travel arrangements, or if other factors increase the amount of time that participants need to decide to attend and make arrangements to register.

The third set of decisions involves who should do the marketing. Again, the best decision depends on a number of situational factors, which may point to anything from a brochure produced on an office copier from text typed by a secretary to a glossy product designed with the assistance of a copywriter and a graphic artist that has typeset text, four-color illustrations, and so forth. For something like the latter, planners would be prudent to allocate six weeks or more for production.

Pitfalls in Marketing the Workshop. Planners who leave their marketing efforts in the hands of someone else and assume that deadlines will be met are risking their entire workshop. Although exceptions occur, the prudent planner follows the rule that unexpected delays are a routine fact of life. Thus, planners who rely on someone else's services should make it a practice to monitor progress weekly and build in time for the inevitable delays. Additional useful guidelines on the marketing of continuing education programs can be found in Farlow (1979), Lenz (1980), and Kotler (1982).

Conducting the Workshop. The actual workshop is to the planning process what opening night is to a play. The curtain goes up when on-site registration for the workshop begins. Because of the short timeframe that characterizes the workshop, planners have little opportunity to correct oversights or make changes. Unfortunately, if a problem develops during the workshop — for example, if a meal is late in being served — that one detail can undermine participants' confidence in the planner's skills, although the planning may otherwise have been impeccable. Workshop managers need to be pragmatic and realize that even errors, slipups, or problems caused by someone else will be seen as their responsibility.

Conducting successful workshops requires meticulous attention to detail. Checklists developed on a quiet day well before the workshop can be an enormous aid here. For workshops of complex design, CPMs not only of the tasks leading up to the event but of the event itself may be a boon to the neophyte or nervous planner. A suggestion that bears consideration is having a staff person on hand during the entire workshop whose sole responsibility is to solve problems that develop during the program. If this is not possible, the planner should try to be present at the beginning and the end of the workshop and if possible at intervals throughout its course to monitor the event. To continue with the theatrical metaphor, one reason for being present at the end of a workshop is to observe the curtain's coming down. Even if there have been problems, participants will leave more well disposed if they have had a chance to express their dissatisfactions to the planner, particularly if the planner expresses gratitude for the feedback. Other guidelines for conducting workshop activities can be found in Davis (1974).

Evaluating the Workshop. Chapter Five of this volume provides ample coverage of this aspect of workshop planning, so it will not be discussed here.

Closing Thoughts

If there is a key to becoming a successful workshop manager, it lies in privately adopting a pessimistic attitude about the smoothness of planning efforts. The successful planner is mentally prepared for problems and sets aside enough time to correct problems so that he or she will not experience undue stress. Lewin's (1947) force field analysis is an excellent strategem for workshop managers. In proceeding through the planning process, the planner can identify forces that will assist him or her to perform tasks to the appropriate standard of quality and forces that can hinder successful completion of those tasks. Experienced continuing educators try to anticipate both kinds of forces and take appropriate action. Being aware of the hindering forces, taking action that gives them the least opportunity to develop, and having emergency plans ready when they appear may be what separates the novice from the veteran workshop planner.

Fatalism can be helpful once the workshop has actually begun. When all else fails, a sense of humor, acknowledgement that the best-laid plans can be frustrated by Murphy's Law, and a cheerful countenance are healthier than fussing, lamenting, or excessive apologizing. The workshop leader will be able to concentrate on helping participants to learn if he or she is reassured that all the nonteaching functions are being taken care of by a planner who demonstrates calm confidence.

References

Buskey, J. H., and Sork, T. J. "From Chaos to Order in Program Planning: A System for Selecting Models and Ordering Research." In *Proceedings from the Twenty-Third Annual Adult Education Research Conference.* Lincoln: Department of Adult and Continuing Education, University of Nebraska, 1982.

Davis, L. N. *Planning, Conducting, and Evaluating Workshops.* Austin, Texas: Learning Concepts, 1974.

Farlow, H. *Publicizing and Promoting Programs.* New York: McGraw-Hill, 1979.

Kotler, P. *Marketing for Nonprofit Organizations.* (2nd ed.) Englewood Cliffs, N.J.: Prentice-Hall, 1982.

Lenz, E. *Creating and Marketing Programs in Continuing Education.* New York: McGraw-Hill, 1980.

Lewin, K. "Frontiers in Group Dynamics: Concept, Method, and Reality in Social Science." *Human Relations,* 1947, *1,* 5–41.

Nadler, L., and Nadler, Z. *The Conference Book.* Houston: Gulf, 1977.

Pennington, F. C. (Ed.). *Assessing Educational Needs of Adults.* New Directions in Continuing Education, no. 7. San Francisco: Jossey-Bass, 1980.

Shipp, T. (Ed.). *Creative Financing and Budgeting.* New Directions for Continuing Education, no. 16. San Francisco: Jossey-Bass, 1982.

Strother, G. B., and Klus, J. P. *Administration of Continuing Education.* Belmont, Calif.: Wadsworth, 1982.

Wilson, J. P. (Ed.). *Materials for Teaching Adults: Selection, Development, and Use.* New Directions for Continuing Education, no. 17. San Francisco: Jossey-Bass, 1983.

Elayne M. Harris is director of extension service at Memorial University, St. John's, Newfoundland. A member of the board of the Canadian Association for Adult Education, she is president-elect of the Canadian Association for University Continuing Education. Prior to her appointment to Memorial, she worked in the Centre for Continuing Education at the University of British Columbia, where she planned and managed the Centre's annual Chautauqua by the Pacific.

Evaluation should focus both on educational value and on effective implementation, using systematic procedures to the extent feasible.

Evaluating Workshop Implementation and Outcomes

Ronald M. Cervero

There is an ongoing debate among continuing educators about the benefits of systematic evaluation of programs. The position taken in this chapter is that determining the worth of a program — the definition of evaluation used here — is such a fundamental human urge that it is done continually at various levels of formality by learners, instructors, and program planners. Since all these individuals make judgments about the worth of all workshops, the issue is not whether workshops should be evaluated but to what degree evaluative information should be collected systematically.

The purpose of this chapter is to provide a framework for the evaluation of workshops that allows readers to consider the types of information that are required to make the desired evaluative judgments and to decide how that information can be collected. First, I present a rationale for the framework. Second, I describe seven types of evaluation and present some sample evaluation questions for each type. Third, I describe and illustrate five criteria that can be used when deciding what type or types of evaluation should be conducted for a workshop.

T. J. Sork (Ed.). *Designing and Implementing Effective Workshops.*
New Directions for Continuing Education, no. 22. San Francisco: Jossey-Bass, June 1984.

Rationale for the Framework

Until the 1960s, the evaluation process developed by Tyler (1950), which focused on determining the congruence between learner outcomes and program objectives, was predominant. Today, this process represents one possible approach of many, with approximately forty formal evaluation models represented in the published literature (Nevo, 1983). Most of these models have at least some applicability to continuing education, as Grotelueschen (1980) has shown in a comprehensive review article. Continuing educators have also written extensively about program evaluation, usually within the context of program planning. The sourcebook edited by Knox (1979a) is particularly rich in information about the evaluation of impact in various continuing education settings.

Such work as Grotelueschen's (1980) provides detailed descriptions of the process of planning and conducting evaluations. Many continuing educators have read that work or similar material, and they have had experience in conducting evaluations within their own work settings. For these reasons, this chapter focuses on a framework for organizing evaluative questions and on creating designs that allow those questions to be answered. As Sork notes in Chapter One, the workshop has two characteristics that distinguish it from other formats: its short timeframe and its focus on identification of problems by learners. The framework described here appears to be particularly well suited to designing evaluations of workshops.

This framework has several antecedents in the literature. Suchman (1967) wrote from the perspective of an evaluation specialist, while Kirkpatrick (1967), Bennett (1975), and Houle (1980) are continuing educators who deal respectively with the fields of training, cooperative extension, and continuing professional education. The framework used in this chapter adapts many of the ideas described in the literature and suggests seven categories of evaluative questions organized around the following criteria: workshop design and implementation; learner participation; learner satisfaction; learner knowledge, skills, and attitudes; application of learning after the workshop; the impact of application of learning; and workshop characteristics associated with outcomes.

This framework should be viewed as a hierarchy only in the sense that evaluative information gathered at one level should not be used to infer success or failure at higher levels. For example, even if learners enjoy a workshop, we cannot infer that their satisfaction was accompanied by changes in knowledge, skills, or attitudes. Although it generally is more costly and difficult to collect evaluative information at the higher levels, this is not always the case. There are many ways of defining a workshop's effectiveness, and the framework described here organizes these ways into seven categories. Yet, the reader should not infer that the evaluative information collected in any one category is inherently better or more useful than information collected in any other. The problem of how to select one or more of the seven types of evaluation is addressed in the last section.

Categories of Evaluation

In this section, the seven categories of evaluation are described in terms of the kinds of questions that can be asked and in terms of the designs that can be used to collect the information that answers the questions. A single example will be used to illustrate the questions and the designs: a three-day workshop conducted on site by a community college to help instructors to improve their ability to teach adults.

Workshop Design and Implementation. This category of evaluation includes factors related to quality, such as activities of learners or instructors, characteristics of the setting, and the nature of the teaching-learning transaction. Evaluation questions in this category include: Was all the material covered? How much time was spent on each topic? Did the instructors follow the workshop design? How much time was allocated to participant discussion? Were meals served on time?

Such evaluative questions as these are constantly being asked during the workshop, although more often than not the resulting information is not systematically collected. Three groups — participants, instructors, and program planners — possess a unique vantage point on these questions, and they can use several techniques — questionnaires, interviews, and observational rating scales — to make systematic observations. For example, if we wanted to know whether all the planned topics were covered, how much time was spent on each, and what methods were used, we could ask both the participants and the instructor to complete a questionnaire that dealt with these questions at the end of each day. If the workshop was being offered for the first time, the program planner might wish to be a participant observer and use a rating scale to collect this information. Interviewing several workshop participants at the close of the workshop is another strategy for collecting the same information. Generally, these strategies require a small amount of effort, yet they tend to produce quite useful evaluative data.

This category of evaluation is important because the implementation process almost always contains unknowns that change the workshop design. Consequently, the actual workshop may be quite different from its design on paper. Thus, it becomes important to know how far from the design the workshop has deviated and in what ways. The instructor or the program planner can judge whether the workshop was implemented as planned and whether any adjustments were made that might be incorporated into the design when the workshop is offered again. This category of evaluative questions is often answered with anecdotal information provided by the instructor or collected in hallway conversations with participants. Nevertheless, such information becomes more useful, particularly for the design of future workshops, when it is collected systematically.

Learner Participation. There is both a quantitative and qualitative dimension to the second category of evaluative questions, which assesses learner participation. The quantitative dimension contains probably the most common evaluative question asked of any workshop: How many participants were there? Two other questions on this dimension are related to clientele analysis: Are these the intended participants? Did certain groups of participants participate less than others? The qualitative dimension has what might be called physical as well as psychological components. The physical component suggests such questions as, Did the participants stay for the entire workshop? While the psychological component suggests such questions as, How involved were the participants?

Data collection designs appropriate to these questions are relatively simple. A record of how many participants attended the activity is usually available either through the formal registration process or from a sign-up sheet. Comparing actual with expected participation characteristics is also easy. For example, if half of the learners were expected to be mathematics professors (because their department expressed the most concern about teaching adults) and no mathematics professors attended, then a clear planning problem has been revealed. The qualitative dimension of participation could be measured by asking the instructor to complete a brief questionnaire or to write a narrative statement at the end of each day's session. A participant observer — either a learner or the program planner — could also provide this information.

With learner satisfaction, this category of evaluation is that most commonly used. Although learner participation is often overemphasized in judgments of workshop quality, it is important for three reasons: First, a minimum level of participation is often required to justify offering the program. Second, the number of participants in a workshop can affect its quality — too few participants or too many are usually detrimental. Third, the extent to which participants are actively engaged in the workshop can influence its effectiveness.

Learner Satisfaction. One common approach in assessing the quality of a workshop is to determine how it is judged by participants. These judgments are based on participants' subjective impressions, and they can focus on many aspects of the workshop, including content, educational process, instructor, physical facilities, and cost. Here are some typical questions: In general, do you think the topics were adequately covered? Did the sequencing of topics promote effective learning? To what extent was the instructor organized? Was the physical environment conducive to learning? Although information required to answer this type of question is often collected anecdotally, use of a systematic method can increase confidence in its validity and reliability. One method involves selecting a representative sample of participants from the total group. This is often the most effective if participants select their own representatives — usually between three and five — at the beginning of the workshop. This representative group can provide continuous evaluation throughout the workshop regarding issues of interest to instructor and participants. The members of this group can be asked to keep their eyes and ears open for reactions from other learners, to poll their fellow learners systematically, to react to evaluative questions on the basis of their own perceptions, or to engage in any combination of these activities.

Perhaps the most common method is the end-of-workshop questionnaire, in which participants respond to a series of open-ended or fixed-response questions. Grotelueschen (1980) presents a variety of questionnaire formats that can be used for this purpose. The primary benefits of this method are that is relatively inexpensive and that responses can be anonymous. Anonymity of responses is important in evaluation, because it reduces the likelihood of bias toward socially desirable responses. A potentially serious weakness of this method is that the validity of evaluative information depends largely on the quality of the questionnaire's construction. Questions that are interpreted by respondents in different ways produce useless data. Kidder (1981) presents a detailed guide to questionnaire construction that should increase the validity and reliability of any data collected.

One of the most sophisticated approaches to assessment of learner satisfaction has been described by Kenny and Harnisch (1982). The Participation Reasons Scale (PRS) contains thirty items designed to assess professionals' reasons for participation. It requires about ten minutes for completion, and it is administered at the beginning of the workshop. The Participation Benefits Scale (PBS) contains items from the PRS with verbs changed to the past tense. It is administered at workshop's end. The pre- and postworkshop data are compared item by item to determine whether the participants' reasons for participation were fulfilled.

Although this category of evaluative questions is important, it is wise for two reasons to interpret learner satisfaction data cautiously, especially when no other evaluative data are collected. First, the questionnaire method is used so frequently that participants are apt to give little thought to their answers. However, collecting the data in two or more ways increases the validity of conclusions about the workshop. The second reason involves a more intractable problem: Studies have shown that learner satisfaction can be unrelated or even negatively related to achievement (Houle, 1980). Thus, when basing generalizations about workshop effectiveness on this category of evaluative data, we must be certain not to infer that participant satisfaction or happiness is a surrogate for learning. On the positive side, these evaluative questions are important because it is common knowledge that learners have different reasons for participating and different preferences for learning format. Thus, success can have multiple definitions within a single workshop, and learner satisfaction data can reveal the variety of definitions or criteria that are used to judge the program.

Learner Knowledge, Skills, and Attitudes. This category of evaluative questions focuses on changes in the learner's cognitive, affective, or psychomotor competence. In evaluating the workshop for community college instructors, the questions in this category could include: Did the participants develop an understanding of the types of learning styles that adults will exhibit in their classrooms? Did the participants change their attitude that adult students are less capable than eighteen-and nineteen-year-old students? Have the participants learned how to lead small groups effectively?

The designs for this type of evaluation have been highly developed for conventional forms of schooling, and they can be summarized in the following way (Houle, 1980): The workshop objectives are stated in terms of what the learner is expected to know or to be able to do at the end. Often, these terms are behavioral, so that the accomplishment of objectives can either be evaluated directly or give rise to evaluation criteria. A system of measurement is devised that permits such evaluation. This system often includes a pretest to determine participants' knowledge or ability at entry. The same measurement is made at the end of the workshop, and the pre- and posttest data are compared to determine whether change has occurred. Judgments are then made about the effectiveness of the workshop. This basic framework was first described formally by Tyler (1950), and it has been widely used since then.

The method of measurement used most often is the paper-and-pencil test. Test development is a complex endeavor. Gronlund (1982) provides a useful set of procedures for constructing achievement tests in the cognitive domain. Kidder (1981) presents a variety of methods for assessing attitudes, including questionnaires, interviews, projective tests, play techniques, psychodrama, and sociodrama. Each of these methods has its strengths and weaknesses, which must be considered when choosing among them. Green and Walsh (1979) describe several techniques for assessing changes in skills, such as role playing in a simulated environment and use of videotapes and motion pictures. It should be noted that these evaluation techniques provide information only about what participants can do in settings divorced from real life.

Conventional wisdom in the field of continuing education suggests that testing is inconsistent with sound principles of adult education. This attitude may have arisen from the extensive use of testing procedures in formal schooling settings and from the fact that continuing educators wish to disassociate themselves from the negative practices of schooling. I believe there is nothing inherently inconsistent or unsound in the use of testing to evaluate continuing education workshops. Testing can be accomplished well or poorly, it can threaten learners or reinforce learning in the workshop, it can be a natural part of the learning process or a contrived barrier to learning, and it can precipitate negative memories of schooling or meet the universal need for feedback. Thus, the important issue is not testing per se but rather the methods used to collect the information, the relationship between the testing process and the educational process, and the intended and actual uses of the information obtained.

Application of Learning After the Workshop. Workshops are temporary and artificial environments that require learners to remove themselves from their natural environment—job, home, community, and so forth—to acquire new capabilities. This category of evaluative questions addresses the degree to which knowledge, skills, and attitudes learned during the workshop can be applied in the learner's natural environment. If the workshop helped participants to acquire new knowledge, is that knowledge reflected in their behavior in their natural environment? For the community college workshop that we are using as an example, the following questions could be posed: Do the faculty who participate demonstrate a positive attitude in the classroom toward the learning capabilities of their adult students? Are they using teaching methods that are consistent with the learning styles of adult students?

The evaluative information in this category is almost always collected after the workshop. Unlike testing, in which the evaluator controls the conditions under which data are collected, assessments of application are much more difficult to control. Thus, we must wait until workshop participants have produced enough data in the natural setting to gather the information that we want. Thus, the community college instructors could be tested for their knowledge gain at the end of the workshop, but we can collect evaluative information on the application of their learning only after they have taught a class that includes adult learners.

Three methods of data collection can be used: self-reports, observation, and archival analysis. Asking participants to describe the extent to which they have applied their learnings from the workshop is the least costly method, but it also produces the least valid results. With the community college instructors, we could either send them a questionnaire or interview them by telephone or in person to learn how they were now teaching. If the workshop encouraged the use of small group discussion, we could ask them to compare the extent to which they were now using this method with the extent to which they used it before the workshop. For a variety of reasons, self-report data need to be interpreted cautiously (Kidder, 1981).

The second method, observation, can cost much more, but it is potentially more valid. This method is probably more appropriate in the work setting, where issues of privacy are less a problem than they are in people's personal lives. Observations can be most effectively made by the individual's supervisor, coworkers, the evaluator, or those affected by the individual's behavior. The classroom teaching performance of community college instructors could be evaluated by the department chairperson, a trained observer, or students.

The third method, archival analysis, uses written records for evaluative purposes. For example, if physicians attend a workshop on the proper use of antibiotics, their patient records for the three months before and after the workshop can be compared to determine whether they are using antibiotics in the ways suggested at the workshop.

In Chapter Three of this sourcebook, Fox addresses three problems in promoting and evaluating the transfer of learning. First, the workshop itself must possess characteristics conducive to the transfer of learning to the work environment. Second, organizational characteristics can interfere with the transfer of learning from the workshop to the work setting. Third, it is not always possible to objectify workshop outcomes in observable behavior. Nevertheless, if we can deal with these issues effectively, we may be able to make some powerful and important conclusions about the workshop's effectiveness.

Impact of Application of Learning. Evaluative questions in this category focus on what have been called the second-order effects of the workshop (Grotelueschen, 1980). First-order effects are the accomplishments of those who share in the direct experience of the workshop — for example, learners and instructors. Second-order outcomes are once removed from these people. Second-order effects represent the impact of first-order effects on other people or institutions. Here are two questions for the community college example: Did the students of community college faculty who attended the workshop learn more effectively because faculty attended the workshop? Did these students feel more positively about their classroom experiences because their instructors attended the workshop?

The same three data collection methods described in the previous section can be used here. For example, the workshop participants could be asked by a questionnaire or an interview whether their changes in teaching style had had any effects on students. More direct evidence of student impact could be obtained by comparing the test scores or grades of students who took the courses before and after the instructors participated in the workshop. Finally, archival records could be used to determine the number of adult students who enrolled in the classes of these instructors over a three-year time period that included semesters both before and after the workshop. If there were significant increases, it could be inferred that a change in teaching methods to accommodate adult learners had helped to increase the enrollment.

This category of questions is potentially the most important, because it often deals with the ultimate goals of continuing education workshops. Yet, answers to such questions can be the most difficult to obtain. This is not true when the workshop is held at a site where all the participants are employed, because institutional records and other data are close at hand. In the case where participants come from many different locations, evaluating the impact of the application of learning is nearly impossible except by self-report.

The most difficult problem in conducting evaluations for this and the preceding category is whether the effect can be attributed to the workshop. Knox (1979b, p. 118) described the problem succinctly: "General program characteristics can be identified that are likely to contribute to impact. One is that the program deals directly with specific and achievable changes in performance that are important to the adult learner, are amenable to educational influence, and that can be readily documented. The second is that the type and amount of educational intervention is likely to bring about the desired change in performance. . . . Even when these two conditions are met (achievable change, reasonable intervention), it is difficult to conduct an impact study likely to prove the extent and types of benefits attributable to the program and not to other influences." Thus, when attempting to reach conclusions about a workshop's impact on learner performance or about the impact of this performance on the work environment, these limitations must be considered.

Workshop Characteristics Associated with Outcomes. The six categories of evaluative questions just described can be grouped into two other categories: implementation questions, which address issues of workshop design and implementation, learner participation, and learner satisfaction, and outcome questions, which address changes in knowledge, skill, and attitude, application of learning, and impact of application of learning. Implementation questions are useful for determining what happens during the workshop. Outcome questions are useful for determining what happened as a result of the workshop. If evaluation is meant to provide information that can be used to improve the workshop, data from implementation questions ideally should be linked with outcome data. That is, workshop characteristics should be associated with the workshop's positive or negative outcomes. Patton (1978, p. 155) described this linkage: "Where outcomes are evaluated without knowledge of implementation, the results seldom provide direction for action, because the decision maker lacks information about what produced the observed outcomes (or lack of outcomes). This is the 'black box' approach to evaluation: Clients are tested before entering the program and after completing the program, while what happens in between is a black box."

For this category of questions, data collection focuses on linking implementation and outcome information that has already been collected. An example from the community college case will serve to illustrate. Let us hypothesize that learners who are more involved in the workshop are more likely to apply what they learn than learners who are less involved. To test this hypothesis, we could ask the instructor to rate each participant for involvement in the workshop, and we could then measure the extent to which participants were using teaching techniques that they learned at the workshop in their classrooms. To compare these two measures, we could graph participants' involvement on one axis and their use of the new teaching techniques on the other. The type of relationship between these two variables would be readily apparent from the resulting curve. If our hypothesis is correct, we may decide to redesign the workshop to produce even more learner involvement.

It can be argued that the many relationships between program implementation and outcomes make definitive statements linking workshop characteristics with workshop outcomes impossible. This is true. Yet, the alternative is to use the workshop title as the explanatory variable. This is a frequent practice, yet it provides no information about how we can improve the workshop. It seems obvious that some information is better than none, as long as we recognize the limitations of the data.

Criteria for Evaluations

Seven types of evaluative questions have been described in the previous section. Since it is not likely that a single evaluation will encompass all the questions, we can focus now on criteria that we can use to decide what kinds of questions to ask. Five criteria can help the evaluator to think this issue through: First, what is the purpose of the workshop? Second, who needs what information? Third, are there any practical and ethical constraints? Fourth, what resources are available? Fifth, what are the evaluator's values? The evaluator's answers to these five questions will all have an impact on the evaluation questions that he or she asks.

Workshops can have many purposes, as the seven categories of questions show. For example, some workshops are intended to have second-order effects, while others are designed to increase participants' knowledge of a subject. Evaluation questions should address these overall purposes. If the planners intend the workshop to change participants' performance, the questions should focus on the application of learning after the workshop. But, if the workshop's purpose is to change participants' attitudes, the evaluation should focus on that, not on the impact of attitude change on coworkers. Thus, one type of evaluation question is better than another only to the extent that it corresponds to the workshop's purposes.

Any evaluation that is done should be planned so that its results can be used (Patton, 1978). To increase the likelihood that results will be used, the evaluator should determine who would use the information and what kind of information those persons would need. These persons should be involved as much as possible in the design, implementation, and analysis of evaluation results, because their involvement in the process will increase the chances that findings will be used. There are five important groups of information users: workshop participants, the workshop instructor, the program planner, those who finance the learners' attendance (for example, employers), and administrators of the sponsoring institution.

Each group can have different information needs. For example, the instructor may want to know whether learners were satisfied with the workshop. Those who finance the learner's attendance may want to know the second-order impacts, and the program planner may be concerned primarily with the number of participants. The evaluation may need to address all these questions.

There are both practical and ethical constraints on the evaluation process. For instance, workshop participants may not want their performance on the job to be observed, or it may not be feasible to do so for other reasons. A host of ethical considerations affect evaluations; they are discussed in depth by Anderson and Ball (1978).

Grotelueschen (1980) discusses several categories of resources that should be considered in planning an evaluation. The availability of these resources should be determined before the evaluative questions are formulated. These resources include money to pay for supplies and services, staff time for such things as interviews and data analysis, and the expertise needed to conduct the evaluation. The evaluation will consume resources that could be used for other purposes. It is important to ascertain what resources are available and how willing people are to use them for evaluation.

Finally, the evaluator's own preferences and values can have an effect on the type of evaluative questions asked (Anderson and Ball, 1978). The evaluator may have personal preferences regarding the workshop's content or process. If the instructor is the evaluator, he or she will have a particular set of biases regarding the workshop, and he or she may also have helpful insights. Also, some evaluators may feel that one type of analytical technique, such as statistical analysis, is more appropriate than others. Thus, the evaluation questions are posed in such a way that answers can be subjected to statistical analysis. It is impossible for the evaluator to expunge these preferences and values; rather, he or she should make them explicit, so that everyone involved in the evaluation process is aware of their influence.

References

Anderson, S. B., and Ball, S. *The Profession and Practice of Program Evaluation.* San Francisco: Jossey-Bass, 1978.

Bennett, C. "Up the Hierarchy." *Journal of Extension,* 1975, *13,* 7–12.

Green, J. S., and Walsh, P. I. "Impact Evaluation in Continuing Medical Education." In A. B. Knox (Ed.), *Assessing the Impact of Continuing Education.* New Directions for Continuing Education, no. 3. San Francisco: Jossey-Bass, 1979.

Gronlund, N. E. *Constructing Achievement Tests.* (3rd ed.) Englewood Cliffs, N.J.: Prentice-Hall, 1982.

Grotelueschen, A. D. "Program Evaluation." In A. B. Knox and Associates, *Developing, Administering, and Evaluating Adult Education.* San Francisco: Jossey-Bass, 1980.

Houle, C. O. *Continuing Learning in the Professions.* San Francisco: Jossey-Bass, 1980.

Kenny, W. R., and Harnisch, D. E. "A Developmental Approach to Research and Practice in Adult and Continuing Education." *Adult Education,* 1982, *33* (1), 29–54.

Kidder, L. H. *Research Methods in Social Relations.* (4th ed.) New York: Holt, Rinehart and Winston, 1981.

Kirkpatrick, D. L. "Evaluation of Training." In R. L. Craig and J. D. Woody (Eds.), *Training and Development Handbook.* New York: McGraw-Hill, 1967.

Knox, A. B. (Ed.). *Assessing the Impact of Continuing Education.* New Directions for Continuing Education, no. 3. San Francisco: Jossey-Bass, 1979a.

Knox. A. B. "Conclusions About Impact Evaluation." In A. B. Knox (Ed.), *Assessing the Impact of Continuing Education.* New Directions for Continuing Education, no. 3. San Francisco: Jossey-Bass, 1979b.

Nevo, D. "The Conceptualization of Educational Evaluation: An Analytical Review of the Literature." *Review of Educational Research,* 1983, *53* (1), 117–128.

Patton, M. C. *Utilization-Focused Evaluation.* Beverly Hills: Sage, 1978.

Suchman, E. A. *Evaluation Research.* New York: Russell Sage Foundation, 1967.

Tyler, R. W. *Basic Principles of Curriculum and Instruction.* Chicago: University of Chicago Press, 1950.

Ronald M. Cervero is assistant professor of adult education in the Department of Leadership and Educational Policy Studies at Northern Illinois University (DeKalb). He teaches courses on program planning and evaluation, and he is currently engaged in research on the effectiveness of continuing education.

*Appropriate use of technology adds variety to workshops and
provides access to an exciting array of instructional resources.*

Using Technology
to Enhance Learning

John H. Buskey

Today, continuing educators seem to have to consider an overwhelm-
ing array of technological options as they develop program activities.
An explosion of technology has occurred in recent years, making it difficult and expensive to keep up to date with the new developments. Not
only are there many new devices, but a new terminology has also
emerged. Thus, continuing educators find themselves in a situation
that Lloyd Longnion has described very well (Kasworm and Anderson,
1982, p. 89): "The third-wave adult educator is one who will be able to
interact in the learning setting with all the technology to encourage self-
directed learning. We're right on the cutting edge. Either we move
ahead, or we drop the ball." Technology is clearly the in thing these
days, yet it is probably used inappropriately as often as it is not. Like
any other instructional methodology or device, technology should be
used to enhance instruction, not just because it is available.

The purpose of this chapter is to suggest ways in which technology can be used to enhance instruction in workshops. In approach-
ing the topic, O'Sullivan's (1976) definition of the elements of technology provides a useful perspective: Technology is a communications
medium. Multimedia technology uses more than one element to accomplish a single communications task. Audiovisual communications

T. J. Sork (Ed.). *Designing and Implementing Effective Workshops.*
New Directions for Continuing Education, no. 22. San Francisco: Jossey-Bass, June 1984.

applies technology to the art and science of transmitting ideas. This chapter builds on these definitions to focus on principles for the selection and use of technologies, on "participation" or communications continua that can be used to decide what sort of interaction between leader and participants is appropriate, the technologies now available for instructional purposes, and how those technologies can be applied individually or collectively in workshop situations.

Selecting and Using Technologies

Because this sourcebook focuses on workshops, only the technologies that have a direct application to short-term learning situations will be discussed here. Technology has three major applications: as an instructional tool, for demonstration purposes, and for hands-on experiential learning. In preparing this chapter, I reviewed the literature on program planning, adult education methods and techniques, technology, media, and training. This literature, especially the books on program planning and training, tends to list criteria for selection and use that can be applied to most forms of media and technology. Thus, this chapter focuses on general criteria. Special requirements are identified where they exist.

Selecting Technologies. In selecting the technology to be used for a specific workshop, writers in the field seem to agree that the first task is to develop the program and the objectives for instruction. Only after this is accomplished can the most appropriate media and technology be selected.

Following the determination of workshop objectives, planners should consider several criteria in selecting the media and technology to be used and the media and technology should be matched with the outcomes desired for each objective (Laird, 1978; Knowles, 1980). Criteria for selecting media and technology include: the size of the group and the experience of participants with the technology; the size and shape of the instructional space; the nature of the content, the sequencing of content, and the general strategies of instruction; the portability of the equipment and the availability of support technology, such as telephone lines, electrical power, television reception, and so forth; the expertise and the resources available to develop and conduct the program; and the capacity of leaders to use the devices and to understand their advantages and disadvantages. These criteria, which are drawn from the experience of skilled continuing educators, such as Donaldson and Scannell (1978), O'Sullivan (1976), and Houle (1972), emphasize the importance of effective program planning and thorough knowledge of the devices selected.

Using Technologies. "Every method has its own rules of excellence, which must be learned if it is to be performed well" (Houle, 1972, p. 158). Conversely, every method can have a significant negative impact if it is used improperly (Michalak and Yager, 1979). Effective leadership is the key to success in any program. If leaders plan to use media and technology, the extent to which they use it effectively will often determine how successful they are.

Every device, particularly the more complex kinds of devices, requires the operator to develop a high level of proficiency in its use. This is by far the most important criterion in employing technology. A second requirement is that the equipment be set up and fully tested before it is used in the session and before the group occupies the workshop site (Knowles, 1980). The lack of such simple things as a three-prong electrical plug, a telephone extension cord or connector, an electrical extension cord, or electrical outlets has caused very carefully planned sessions to fail. Every experienced workshop leader can cite instances in which some common device either failed or was not available, producing a last-minute scramble for the part or a modification in the instructional plan. Murphy's Law — "Whatever can go wrong will go wrong" — never seems more true than in technological demonstrations. A third requirement, especially with complex media, is to brief students on the purpose of the aid and on what they should look for in the session (Knowles, 1980). Instructors can be so familiar with the devices they use that they forget to help participants to understand how they can benefit from them at the workshop.

Laird (1978) suggests that visual presentations should be unified — that is, they should make one point — and they should be simple, accurate, colorful, legible, and easily visible. While the preceding principles do not apply to all uses of technology, they are important for most uses. In considering technologies for use in workshops and specific sessions, planners can avail themselves of a wealth of information. The guidelines and criteria presented here are general in nature. However, they form a solid basis for program planning and development.

Participation Continua

One key consideration in designing a workshop or other short-term learning program is linking together in an appropriate sequence not only the content of the program but also the situations in which participants and leaders interact. Workshops consist of a series of learning experiences or learning situations that occur in a relatively short period of time. They vary in length from a few hours to a few weeks. Most are less than five days long. Workshops are characterized by the intensity and the variety of interaction patterns among participants and between participants and leaders. One way of looking at workshops and other short-term programs focuses on the human interaction that takes place among the various actors. Experienced planners, particularly those who have an orientation toward human relations training, tend to concentrate on this issue, because they know that program success depends on successful human interaction. As the use of technological devices becomes more prevalent, it is important to consider not only the ways in which people interact with people but also the ways in which people interact with machines in learning situations.

The elements of interaction that should be considered are many and varied, and they differ from program to program, depending on content, leadership, and to some extent facilities. There are several ways of conceptualizing interaction. In this chapter, I will suggest a number of different approaches, and I will recommend that the reader adopt or adapt the concepts that best fit his or her approach to the conduct of workshops.

Most continuing educators are familiar with many of the methods and techniques that are commonly used to provide adults with learning experiences. Such methods can be viewed as forms of communication patterns or interaction processes among people. When viewed as patterns or processes, methods can be organized on a continuum. When they are so organized, they can be related to one another. Such a continuum can be a powerful tool for the program planner in selecting and designing learning experiences for adults.

Several writers have proposed continua that describe what happens in the learning situation. By situation, we mean a specific period of time — perhaps an hour, perhaps a half day. The situation or session has an identifiable beginning and ending, and it usually features one method or technique or interaction. When the interaction patterns are placed in the order in which they occur in the workshop, we have a comprehensive view of how and when people communicate with each other.

Figure 1 illustrates one conceptualization of the organization of interaction processes. The model has three important characteristics: It is a bipolar continuum, it is based on the flow of direct communication among all actors in the learning situation, and the communication patterns are organized in a particular sequence on the basis of specific principles.

At one end of the continuum is a didactic, lecture-type situation in which teachers or instructors have full control of the learning situation, and participants listen passively. Communication is one-way,

Figure 1. Interaction Processes

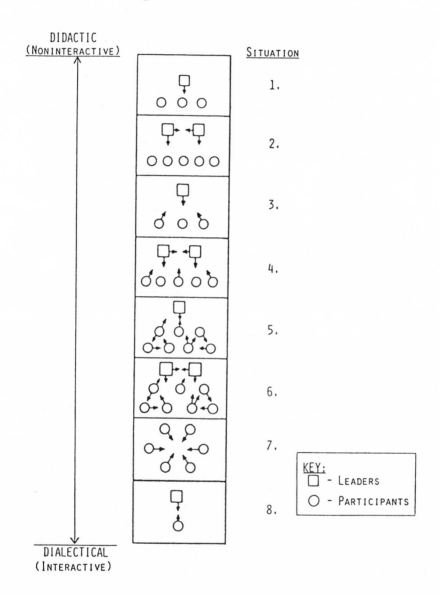

from teacher or device to learners. This situation represents the non-interactive pole, and technological devices associated with it include film, transparency and video projectors, television, and audiotapes.

Toward the other, or dialectical, end of the continuum, communication flows among all present (such as in a face-to-face discussion group), responsibility for the activity rests fully on all present, and each person has an opportunity for extensive participation. This situation represents the interactive pole, and such technological devices as the telephone, two-way television, and computer-based instruction can be used to provide participants with direct interaction.

Three principles organize this continuum: Learners are passive (or noninteractive) at the didactic pole and become increasingly more active as we move toward the dialectical pole (Berelson and Steiner, 1964; Ginther, 1965). Communication is one-way at the didactic pole and becomes more open or diverse as we move toward the dialectical pole (Verner, 1962). Responsibility for initiation and direction of the interaction shifts from the leader in the didactic situation to the learner in the dialectical or interactive situation (Buskey, 1970).

Although the continuum of interaction patterns was developed to describe personal interaction, it applies equally well to the selection and use of technological and audiovisual devices. As each device is considered, the pattern that it would establish can be identified on the continuum, and its appropriateness can be determined. The continuum can also be used to determine the variety of interaction or communication patterns used in individual sessions in a specific program.

Another way of looking at participation in learning situations involves something called *degree of abstraction*. First proposed by Dale (1954) and later adapted by Knowles (1980) and Laird (1978), Dale's "cone of experience" defines ten points along a continuum ranging from abstract to concrete. At the abstract end of the continuum are verbal and visual symbols, such as books, teaching machine programs, charts, and diagrams; at the concrete end of the continuum are contrived and direct experiences, such as models, specimens, work manuals, or observation guides. A similar continuum has been described by Verner (1962), who defined five reference points: abstract pole, semiabstract, somewhat removed, direct experience, and concrete direct experience.

A planning group can use the interaction patterns continuum and the degree of abstraction continuum to discuss alternative methods or devices. As planners consider each technological device, they can judge the extent to which it provides concrete experiences and fosters active involvement and face-to-face communication among participants. Ways in which these patterns can be used in describing program situations are illustrated in the first case study presented later in this chapter. Neither continuum implies that one level or point is better or more valuable than another. The continua simply define various ways in which learning situations can be described.

Specific Technologies

Many different technological devices can be used to enhance the learning process. By device, I mean a specific machine. Although many devices can be used alone, it is becoming more common to link machines together in order to develop more powerful instructional systems. In fact, the number of ways in which devices can be linked is limited only by the imagination of the workshop leader.

Specialists in telecommunications have recently attempted to categorize the major technologies in order to analyze the variety of ways in which organizations are using various devices and systems. As Table 1 shows, Lewis (1983) first divides them into noninteractive and interactive technologies. The noninteractive technologies, "when used alone, permit communication in only one direction (for example, broadcast radio and television)" (Lewis, 1983, p. 29). The interactive technologies permit some form of two-way communication, such as two-way audio systems and computer conferencing. Interaction was chosen as the organizing concept for the framework because it is directly pertinent to the educator's interests in teacher-student, student-student, and student-material interaction and in the student's control over the use of the media. As a practical concept, it also fits well with the participation continua discussed earlier in this chapter. In Table 1, the devices themselves have been placed in three categories: audio, video, and computer. Note that a device or system can be considered either interactive or noninteractive, depending on how it is configured.

Table 1. Telecommunications Technologies

	Noninteractive	*Interactive*
Audio	Radio Audiotape	Telephone Audio teleconferencing

Video	Open-broadcast television
	Cable television (one-way)
	Videotape
	Instructional Television
	  Fixed Service (ITFS)
	Satellite television (one-way)
	Slow scan/freeze-frame
	  television (one-way)
		Microwave (point-to-point)
		Cable television (two-way)
		Cable television (viewer-response)
		Slow scan/freeze-frame
		  television (two-way)
		Electronic blackboard
		Satellite television (two-way)
		Video teleconferencing

Computer		Computer-assisted instruction Computer-based instructional management

Source: Lewis, 1983, p. 30.

Lewis (1983) lists nineteen different telecommunication technologies, several relate to systems, several are more complex versions of simpler technologies, and several simply have no direct applications in workshops. In addition, some devices often used by workshop leaders, such as projectors, are not included. Thus, in the paragraphs that follow, the focus will be on such basic devices as audio technologies, video technologies, computers, and projectors that have specific applications in workshops.

Audio Devices. The two major audio devices used in workshops are the telephone and audiotape. Patented in 1876 by Alexander Graham Bell, the telephone is probably the most common communications device in use today. Until relatively recently, however, it had not been used extensively for instructional purposes in workshops and other short-term learning activities. By itself, the telephone is a useful device, and it can be used in several ways, but its real potency comes from its ability to link other technological devices together. The telephone system is being used in several ways to provide instruction in workshops.

First, it is the basis for a large number of audio telephone networks. An audio network consists of several phones connected by a common line, either through a bridging switchboard or through a dedicated line system—a sort of party-line that is available twenty-four hours a day. Dedicated line systems usually offer better-quality sound, because only a limited number of phones are connected, and a minimum amount of switching equipment is involved. Each site is equipped with a speaker telephone or an amplifier/microphone arrangement, so that participants can hear what those at other sites are saying and also speak to and be heard by others on the network. By using such a network, a single resource person can conduct several workshops at the same time. Another common use of the telephone is to "bring" a resource person in another city to the workshop. If speaker phones are used at each site, the speaker can deliver a message and respond to questions from the audience. In both these uses, it is helpful for the workshop leaders and speakers to provide support materials that can be used at each delivery site. These materials can be transparencies, printed handouts, newsprint stand materials, or slides.

The telephone system can also be used to transmit computer information, to connect electronic blackboards, to connect slow scan/freeze-frame television signals, and to provide two-way audio communications for one-way video transmission systems. It is a very versatile communications device!

Much of the growing body of literature on the use of technology for educational purposes relates to the telephone. The published proceedings of a recent conference on teleconferencing (Parker and Olgren, 1983) contains reports on more than fifty practical applications of telecommunications, and many reports describe uses of the telephone, either alone or in combination with other devices. The same publication contains a detailed description of all facets of audio teleconferencing. A particularly lucid, practical manual on how to conduct audio teleconferences was written by Monson (1978).

An audiotape recorder/playback machine can be used to play prerecorded audiotapes of music, speeches, presentations, and so forth, and it can also be used to record events in the workshop, either for immediate use or for later playback. When audiotapes are used in programs, the segments played should be brief; otherwise, the session may become tedious for participants. A common use of such machines today is to tape-record workshop and conference presentations for sale to program participants and to people who cannot attend. Both the machine and audiocassette tapes are inexpensive to purchase and simple to operate. Such writers as Laird (1978), Morgan and others (1976), Nadler (1982), and O'Sullivan (1976) provide guidelines and helpful hints on the use of audiotapes in continuing education programs.

Video Technologies. There are many ways in which video can be used in workshops to support interactive or noninteractive learning. The equipment components include video monitors, videotape recorder/playback machines, cameras, switching equipment, and videotapes. A flexible technology, video technology can be used in a self-contained manner within a classroom, or it can be connected through closed circuit or open broadcast systems to origination sites in distant cities.

As a self-contained unit, a video system that includes one or more monitors, a videotape recorder/playback machine, switching equipment, and cameras is frequently used in workshops for recording and playing back live-action workshop activities, such as demonstrations or role-playing exercises. Videotape can also be used to provide presentations prerecorded by speakers who cannot attend the program. On a more limited scale, a video monitor connected to a closed circuit television system or to a videotape recorder/playback machine can be used to show prerecorded programs, much like a movie projector.

On a larger scale, national or regional satellite video conferences can be delivered to many sites simultaneously. Local workshop participants receive segments of the instruction from a live or prerecorded national broadcast, then engage in activities on site that relate the material to their local interests. The video signal can be originated from one or from multiple sites, and it can involve either one-way or two-way transmissions. Frequently, telephone systems are used to provide two-way communications capability, especially when the video signal is only one-way. The National University Teleconferencing Network headquartered at Oklahoma State University and other private and public organizations regularly conduct national programs via satellite on a variety of topics. One emerging technology, videodisc, may become an important instructional tool for continuing education. Each videodisc contains 57,000 individual pictures or frames. With its still-frame, motion, electronic address, rapid-frame address, and computer interface capability, the videodisc possesses considerable potential for group or individualized interactive or noninteractive instruction. Since the technology is still in the research and development phase, the amount of instructional software available for it remains relatively small, but more software should be developed as the technology gains acceptance.

Descriptions of various video applications appear in Lewis (1983), Olgren and Parker (1983), and Parker and Olgren (1983). The use of videotape machines in workshop settings is discussed by O'Sullivan (1976), Wohlking (1976), Morgan and others (1976), and Goldstein (1974).

Computers. Two major forms of computer technology interest workshop planners: time-sharing systems and stand-alone microcomputers. Time-sharing systems connect a remote terminal or microcomputer by direct cable or telephone lines to a mainframe computer or a minicomputer, which can be a few feet or many miles away. Access to some time-sharing systems is limited to a group of specific terminals; other systems, including many national on-line data bases, can be accessed by anyone who pays a membership fee and has the proper equipment and software.

Many universities have computer-assisted instruction (CAI) systems, which allow students to interact directly with a large computer through a terminal. The PLATO system developed by the University of Illinois and Control Data Corporation is one of the better-known systems. In contrast, microcomputers function as self-contained machines and make highly sophisticated computer power available to the general public at low cost. First introduced in 1976, microcomputers have created new instructional opportunities for all levels of education.

Both types of system afford a variety of opportunities for workshop planners, particularly when systems are equipped with such peripheral devices as modems (for communication via the telephone), printers, disk drives, and video monitors. Specific instructional content can be learned; reports can be prepared with word processing, electronic spreadsheet, or database software; remote data bases can be accessed;

games and simulations can be played; and workshop leaders can create their own exercises and activities relevant to the program's content.

The rapid growth of on-line data bases accessible by terminals and microcomputers equipped with modems warrants special attention here, because these technologies represent an unusual resource for workshop planners and leaders. By connecting a microcomputer with the proper software program to a telephone modem, one can access more than 1,350 different computerized data bases across the nation (Glossbrenner, 1983). About 30 percent are free, but most of the more sophisticated data bases exact membership and access time fees. The wealth and diversity of the information available in this way are enormous, which creates the potential for using data bases in workshops dealing with almost any topic.

Information about the use of computers in instructional situations appears in numerous books, journals, and magazines. Garraway (1982) provides a good overview of microcomputers as a teaching technology in adult education. Computer conferencing is discussed by Olgren and Parker (1983). Basic information about programmed instruction and computer-assisted instruction can be found in Brethower (1976) and Hickey (1976).

Projectors. Projectors come in all shapes and sizes to meet the needs of their users. They include movie projectors, overhead transparency projectors, slide projectors, filmstrip projectors, and opaque projectors. Each has its own medium (films, transparencies, slides). However, the workshop leader should be aware that there are many equipment manufacturers and several sizes of slides (35mm, 2 x 2, lantern) and films (16mm, 8mm). Recently, television projectors for large-screen presentations and computer image projectors have become available.

There is a wealth of information on the use of projectors in continuing education programs. The literature from the field of training and development is particularly helpful in suggesting guidelines for use of the different kinds of projectors. O'Sullivan (1976), Laird (1978), Goldstein (1974), and Donaldson and Scannell (1978) all provide information useful for the workshop leader and planner.

Applications of Technologies in Workshops

It is possible to use many of the technological devices just enumerated either alone or in various combinations. Since single applications were addressed in the preceding section, this section contains some case studies that illustrate how several devices can be combined to enhance workshop learning situations.

Simultaneous Workshops at Multiple Sites. Through the use of either a dedicated line or a dial-up audio telephone network, it is possible to conduct workshops or other activities at several sites simultaneously, although the sites may be many miles apart and even in different time zones. Such a program requires substantial advance planning for facilities, human resources, equipment, and instructional materials, and it will probably require some advance training or orientation for workshop leaders at each of the remote sites.

Let us assume that we want to conduct a one-day leadership skills workshop for supervisors in six different cities. One city will serve as the base or primary origination site for one workshop, and the primary workshop leader will operate from this city. The other five cities will be primarily receive sites, although the telephone network makes it possible for any site to originate communications to the other sites.

The equipment needed includes the audio telephone network with appropriate speakers and microphones, videotape playback machines and video monitors, movie projectors, and overhead transparency projectors. Other devices could also be used, but those just named will suffice for the purpose of this case study.

In carrying out the program, each local workshop leader will take a few minutes to assemble the group, ask participants to introduce themselves, and distribute materials. The primary leader will then originate the first session on the network, introducing the day's topic and making an oral presentation that may last an hour. This talk can be based on printed topical or outline materials that participants receive before the workshop, or it can be accompanied by carefully cued and synchronized overhead transparencies that the local leaders show at each site. The resulting interaction format is similar to that shown in situation one of Figure 1. A few minutes can be set aside for a brief question-and-answer period, which is represented by situation three of Figure 1.

Following this session, participants at each local site can view a videotape of a case study or situation that illustrates one or more key points made in the oral presentation. The local groups can then hold group discussions (situation seven, in Figure 1) in order to develop understanding and identify questions for a subsequent panel discussion.

That panel, comprised of the primary and local workshop leaders, can respond to questions from participants at all sites. Participants at site six may want to ask a question of the leader at site three, and so forth. In this way, all sites can gain access to the expertise of a leader or participant at any one of the local sites. This interaction format is similar to that described by situation five and six of Figure 1.

Other workshop sessions can consist of presentations over the network by primary or local workshop leaders, films or slide presentations, and various kinds of group activities. The program can switch periodically from local activities to network activities, depending on the program design.

Once the leaders have been trained and the original materials and necessary equipment have been acquired, a popular topic can be offered many times in locations convenient to participants at very reasonable cost. A variety of interactive situations can be created and participants and leaders can be involved in a productive workshop. There are four keys to successful programs: trained leaders who are not only knowledgeable in the subject matter but skillful and confident in using the technology as well, advance planning, variety in presentation style, and alternative plans in case a technological problem develops.

A Video Teleconference. Sponsored by the American University of Washington, D.C., and the University of Nebraska–Lincoln, a satellite video teleconference titled "Productivity in America" was carried on the National University Teleconferencing Network in January 1983. A one-day conference, it attracted 1,200 enrollments at forty institutions across the country. The program featured four internationally known faculty experts on productivity from the two sponsoring institutions.

The program began with an hour-long live presentation by an expert on economic productivity from American University. His talk, which originated from the campus in Washington, was up-linked to the Westar IV satellite, then transmitted to receive sites at the forty local institutions. It was followed at the local sites by group discussions led by local economics and management faculty, who tailored their sessions to productivity problems common to local business and industry. The local discussions were based on extensive written case study materials prepared in advance by the four faculty resource people.

Later in the day, a second telecast from the University of Nebraska-Lincoln featured a three-man panel of experts on Japanese and American approaches to productivity improvement. This segment was broadcast live from studios in Lincoln and up-linked to the same satellite. Following the presentation, small groups at each receive site discussed the day's presentations and developed specific questions to be addressed to the four resource persons. Each local group then telephoned its questions to staff in the Lincoln studios.

The third telecast of the day was a live question-and-answer period originating from both Lincoln and Washington. The panel moderator read the questions on the air or the questioner was put on the air live, and the session was switched back and forth between Washington and Lincoln, depending on the resource person who answered the question. A final wrap-up session at each site was conducted by local faculty.

To deal with the problem of four time zones, the two major presentations were telecast live to the Eastern and Central time zones and taped for rebroadcast to the Mountain and Pacific zones. The question-and-answer session was conducted twice: once for the eastern zones and once for the western zones.

Such an undertaking involves a great deal of coordination, major television studios, satellite up-link transmitters, and long-range planning for the origination and production sites. The receive sites required satellite dishes to receive the signals, video monitors or large-screen video projectors, and telephones. A number of sites used other audiovisual equipment. Some institutions used existing satellite receivers, and others rented them for the day.

Computers in Workshops. There are many ways in which computers can be used as tools for instruction. For the purposes of illustration, let us assume that we want to conduct a workshop on marketing for agribusiness managers that teaches them how to trade in the commodities market. In order to make the learning situation both realistic and participative, we want to teach them how to gather current data about commodities, how to analyze those data, and how to make decisions about buying and selling such commodities as corn, wheat, and soybeans.

The equipment that we require includes a touchtone telephone connected to a clear line (preferably not through a local switchboard), a microcomputer with two disk drives, a modem to connect the computer with the telephone, communications software (which may come with the modem), a printer connected to the computer, several large twenty-five-inch video monitors on stands, and appropriate cables. In order to make the exercise go smoothly, the workshop leader should test the equipment before the session begins.

One of the items that workshop participants need for the exercise is the current prices of commodities. One way of obtaining such data is to access a commodity data base, such as the Commodities News Service (CNS), which tracks news and price activity on all major commodity exchanges. Prices are updated every ten minutes. CNS is available on The Source, an on-line data base owned by the *Reader's Digest* company that is probably the best known and largest of many information utilities now accessible by microcomputers through modems and long-distance telephone lines. CNS is also available on other information utilities (Glossbrenner, 1983).

To use the system, we must subscribe to The Source, set up an account, and receive various documents that describe how to use the system. To operate the system for this exercise, the leader or an aide will make a telephone call to The Source, log on to the CNS data base, and request the information necessary for the exercise: for example, the current prices of various grades of corn, wheat, and soybeans. The data can then be displayed on the video monitors for use by participants in the exercise. Alternatively, the printer can be used to produce hard copy, which can be duplicated on office photocopying machines — another useful device for workshop members. This process can be repeated several times during the workshop to demonstrate the hourly or daily fluctuation in prices and the consequences of buy or sell decisions at specific times.

Given the number and variety of the available data bases, the possibilities for use in workshops are nearly endless. For example, in a recent workshop in which I was involved, we accessed the *Catalog of Federal Domestic Assistance* data base to demonstrate to community leaders how to generate a list of potential federal funding agencies for a specific community project.

Conclusion

The use of technology to enhance learning in workshops or other short-term learning situations is in one sense still in its infancy but in another is well into maturity. Technology is changing so rapidly that new options seem to become available almost daily. Yet, many of the principles for selecting and using technologies in learning situations have been well tested and need only be applied with imagination and creativity in order to plan and conduct effective workshops.

References

Berelson, B., and Steiner, G. A. *Human Behavior: An Inventory of Scientific Findings.* New York: Harcourt Brace and World, 1964.

Brethower, K. S. "Programmed Instruction." In R. L. Craig (Ed.), *Training and Development Handbook.* (2nd ed.) New York: McGraw-Hill, 1976.

Buskey, J. H. "The Development and Testing of a Typology of Adult Education Programs in University Residential Centers." Unpublished doctoral dissertation, University of Chicago, 1970.

Dale, E. *Audiovisual Methods in Teaching.* New York: Dryden, 1954.

Donaldson, L., and Scannell, E. E. *Human Resource Development: The New Trainer's Guide.* Reading, Mass.: Addison-Wesley, 1978.

Garraway, H. "The Development of a Unique Teaching Technology." In D. G. Gueulette (Ed.), *Microcomputers for Adult Learning: Potentials and Pitfalls.* Chicago: Follett, 1982.

Ginther, J. R. "A Conceptual Model for Analyzing Instruction" In J. P. Lysaught (Ed.), *Programmed Instruction in Medical Education.* Rochester, N.Y.: Rochester Clearinghouse, University of Rochester, 1965.

Glossbrenner, A. *The Complete Handbook of Personal Computer Communications.* New York: St. Martin's Press, 1983.

Goldstein, I. L. *Training: Program Development and Evaluation.* Monterey, Calif.: Brooks/Cole, 1974.

Hickey, A. E. "Computer-Assisted and Computer-Managed Instruction." In R. L. Craig (Ed.), *Training and Development Handbook.* (2nd ed.) New York: McGraw-Hill, 1976.

Houle, C. O. *The Design of Education.* San Francisco: Jossey-Bass, 1972.

Kasworm, C. E., and Anderson, C. A. "Perceptions of Decision Makers Concerning Microcomputers for Adult Learning." In D. G. Gueulette (Ed.), *Microcomputers for Adult Learning: Potentials and Pitfalls.* Chicago: Follett, 1982.

Knowles, M. S. *The Modern Practice of Adult Education.* (Rev. ed.) Chicago: Association Press/Follett, 1980.

Laird, D. *Approaches to Training and Development.* Reading, Mass.: Addison-Wesley, 1978.

Lewis, R. J. *Meeting Learners' Needs Through Telecommunications: A Directory and Guide to Programs.* Washington, D.C.: Center for Learning and Telecommunications, American Association for Higher Education, 1983.

Michalak, D. F., and Yager, E. G. *Making the Training Process Work.* New York: Harper & Row, 1979.

Monson, M. *Bridging the Distance: An Instructional Guide to Teleconferencing.* Madison: Instructional Communications Systems, University of Wisconsin Extension, 1978.

Morgan, B., Holmes, G. E., and Bundy, C. E. *Methods in Adult Education.* Danville, Ill.: Interstate, 1976.

Nadler, L. *Designing Training Programs: The Critical Events Model.* Reading, Mass.: Addison-Wesley, 1982.

Olgren, C. H., and Parker, L. A. *Teleconferencing Technology and Applications.* Dedham, Mass.: Artech House, 1983.

O'Sullivan, K. "Audiovisuals and the Training Process." In R. L. Craig (Ed.), *Training and Development Handbook.* (2nd ed.) New York: McGraw-Hill, 1976.

Parker, L. A., and Olgren, C. H. *Teleconferencing and Electronic Communications II: Applications, Technologies, and Human Factors.* Madison: Center for Interactive Programs, University of Wisconsin Extension, 1983.

Verner, C. *A Conceptual Scheme for the Identification and Classification of Processes.* Chicago: Adult Education Association of the U.S.A., 1962.

Wohlking, W. "Role Playing." In R. L. Craig (Ed.), *Training and Development Handbook.* (2nd ed.) New York: McGraw-Hill, 1976.

John H. Buskey is associate dean of the Division of Continuing Studies and assistant professor in the Department of Adult and Continuing Education at the University of Nebraska–Lincoln. He has planned and conducted hundreds of workshops, and he has a particular interest in program planning and evaluation.

*Some thoughts on the future of workshops and sources
for further reading are offered.*

Postscript and Prologue

Thomas J. Sork

The typical image that comes to mind when we hear the word *workshop*
is of a group of people seated at tables within a room. Surrounded by
sheets of newsprint taped to the wall, they are engaged in discussion
under the watchful eye of an expert leader. Yet, the definition of workshop presented in Chapter One can accommodate some very different
images. For example, a workshop can also consist of twenty individuals
each sitting at home communicating with one another and the workshop leader via computer terminals and telephone or coaxial cable lines.
The interaction in this situation may be purely verbal (written and
spoken words), or it may also have a nonverbal component (two-
dimensional or holographic images). Although the media of interaction
are different in the two cases, the nature of the interaction and the
resulting outcomes can be the same.

Bringing people together to pursue learning objectives has until
recently meant physically moving them to a central location where the
instructional resources and leadership have been assembled. Yet, the
technologies discussed in Chapter Six now provide us with the means
to bring learners together electronically — potentially a much more
powerful and economical technique. It can be argued that the face-to-
face interaction which takes place when people travel to a central location is an essential ingredient of effective problem solving. But, even if

T. J. Sork (Ed.). *Designing and Implementing Effective Workshops.*
New Directions for Continuing Education, no. 22. San Francisco: Jossey-Bass, June 1984.

this perspective is correct, the technologies available today make it possible to retain most of the features of face-to-face interaction while adding important new dimensions to the learning experience. For example, an electronic assembly of people allows participation from anywhere on earth that enriches the workshop experience by involving individuals with quite different backgrounds and experiences. And, if the assumption that face-to-face interaction is essential for effective learning is ill-founded, then the advantages of electronic assembly become even more attractive.

Problems of compatibility, which are always a concern when people come together for the first time, remain a formidable barrier when people are brought electronically. Although personal compatibility will continue to be an issue, there is hope that the issue of electronic compatibility will become moot, since the potential commercial rewards for developing compatible "compunications" technologies are so great. But, the continuing bias toward group instruction that we find in the literature on continuing education and in the programs that prepare practitioners remains a barrier to effective tests of the "electronic workshop." Little theoretical work has been done on how continuing educators can incorporate new technologies into programs, on the advantages and disadvantages associated with such changes, and on the effects that new technologies will have on learning outcomes. It is unclear how widely these technologies will be accepted as tools for learning. Much will depend on their perceived effectiveness and ease of use. But, it would seem prudent for those involved in continuing education to keep up to date with developments and to consider how widespread adoption of these technologies would affect the design and delivery of programs.

The first five chapters in this volume were based on the assumption that participants would be brought together physically, because that is how most workshops are now organized. But, it is interesting to consider how this sourcebook would have to be changed if a significant number of workshops were to use electronic media. Consider, for example, how Chapter Two, which described ways of creating participatory, task-oriented learning environments, would look if the medium of interaction were electronic. What techniques would be required to assure that participants in an electronic interaction remained engaged and interested in the activities? What skills would the workshop leader responsible for the interaction require? Or, consider Chapter Three, on transfer of learning to the work environment. What effect would electronic interaction have on the probability of transfer of learning? What methods for fostering transfer would be most effective in the electronic workshop? Chapter Four deals with planning and management tasks. What new skills would those who plan and manage electronic workshops require, and what new steps would have to be added to the planning process? Evaluation, the topic of Chapter Five, would be especially challenging in an electronic-mediated workshop. The absence of physical contact with participants would require a new approach to data collection. What happens to the traditional approaches to evaluation in a world of computer-mediated learning? And, with such powerful tools available to monitor learner performance and opinion, who will be responsible for assuring that the information is used in an ethical manner and that the interests and rights of participants are protected?

Clearly, recent developments in electronic technology have provided continuing educators with much to think about. On the face of it, the primary response to these developments by those involved in continuing education seems to have been to provide programs that enable adults to learn about the technology. In the near-term future, however, there may be increasing demand for programs designed to teach adults how to learn using the technology, and this development may be followed by programs designed to promote learning through the technology.

These are indeed interesting times in which to be a continuing educator — times that require careful consideration of both the options available and of the consequences of choosing each option. The workshop format is one option open to those who plan continuing education programs. This sourcebook has provided information that should help those interested in designing and implementing workshops to undertake the task in a more thoughtful and effective way. In the remainder of this chapter, I will describe some other publications on the various aspects of workshop planning and delivery that complement and supplement the ideas presented here. Publications in the first group address the design and implementation of workshops, although the author's implicit or explicit definitions of workshop are often quite different from the definition that informs this sourcebook. Books in the second group do not directly address issues related to workshops, but what they say seems to apply to many tasks that workshop planners encounter.

Books on Workshop Design and Implementation

Beckhard, R. *How to Plan and Conduct Workshops and Conferences.* New York: Association Press, 1956.

One of the first works dealing exclusively with the planning of short-term programs, this book provides detailed nuts-and-bolts procedures for designing and operating conferences and workshops from initial planning through follow-up action.

Cooper, S., and Heenan, C. *Preparing, Designing, and Leading Workshops: A Humanistic Approach.* Boston: CBI, 1980.

These authors describe a process and present a set of principles designed to produce learning experiences that involve learners on the intellectual, emotional, physical, and spiritual dimensions. Although the humanistic approach seems oversold as a unique perspective in continuing education, the authors provide useful, albeit somewhat overgeneralized, guidelines for making planning decisions and for leading workshop activities. This work is especially recommended to the neophyte workshop planner.

Davis, L. N. *Planning, Conducting, and Evaluating Workshops.* Austin, Texas: Learning Concepts, 1974.

Using a breezy, often witty, writing style, the author devotes chapters to each major task of workshop design and implementation. He includes numerous charts, checklists, and forms that workshop planners may find useful for such tasks as assessing needs, writing general and specific objectives, designing instruction, budgeting, and evaluating outcomes. Although based on a somewhat outmoded notion of management styles and a very idiosyncratic set of generalizations about adult learners, Davis's book is a readable and practical guide for workshop planners.

Hart, L. B., and Schleicher, J. G. *A Conference and Workshop Planner's Manual.* New York: AMACOM, American Management Associations, 1979.

Those who find that checklists, forms, diagrams, and charts help them to organize themselves and keep track of planning details will find this book to be of value. In fact, about 70 percent of the book consists of aids to planning; the remaining 30 percent is text. The procedures suggested are based on a loosely defined systems approach to planning. Readers who need help getting organized should take a look at this book. Readers who need help improving the educational effectiveness of workshops should look elsewhere.

Loughary, J. W., and Hopson, B. *Producing Workshops, Seminars, and Short Courses: A Trainer's Handbook.* Chicago: Association Press/ Follett, 1979.

In this well-organized, clearly written book, the authors deal with issues that others often ignore — such as determining whether an educational program will solve the problem or whether another economic, organizational, or personnel approach is required — and they provide useful trainer's tips throughout the volume. Considerable space is devoted to discussions of the human relationships and mutual expectations that develop when a short-term program is used to address performance problems. This book should be useful for neophyte and veteran alike; it is especially suitable for the free-lance or independent workshop planner.

Shenson, H. L. *How to Create and Market a Successful Seminar or Workshop.* Washington, D.C.: Bermont Books, 1981.

According to the author (pp. 9–10), "Success in the seminar and workshop business is much more a function of marketing and promotion than it is the result of program design, materials development, and instructional competency." Whether one agrees with this statement or not, it clearly reveals the orientation of this book. The ideas presented are couched in marketing terminology and range from what days of the week are best for advertising (Sunday for newspapers, Monday for radio) to the proper form for contracts. The suggestions made appear to have their origins in the experiences of the author, so readers should not expect to see evidence or argument to support the practical advice given. This book should be especially useful to the free-lance entrepreneur.

Other Useful Books on Related Topics

Burke, W. W., and Beckhard, R. *Conference Planning.* (2nd ed.) Washington, D.C.: NTL Institute for Applied Behavioral Science, 1970.

This collection of readings is organized around four topics: planning, conference technology, special conferences, and training for group discussion leaders. The authors include such notables as Margaret Mead, Kenneth Benne, Ronald Lippitt, and Leland Bradford. Each essay has clear implications for the conference planner. The first section — on planning — and the last — on training discussion leaders — should be of particular interest to those involved with workshops.

Drain, R. H., and Oakley, N. *Successful Conference and Convention Planning.* Toronto: McGraw-Hill Ryerson, 1978.

This book is written primarily for the planner of large conferences that require a great deal of administrative work. If a workshop that requires a great deal of logistical support (programs for spouses, transportation, awards, and exhibits) is being planned, then this book may be useful. Readers should be warned that the authors assume that planners have a brigade of paid staff or volunteers at their disposal.

Lord, R. W. *Running Conventions, Conferences, and Meetings.* New York: AMACOM, American Management Associations, 1981.

Although this book was written for the business executive, it can be useful for the workshop planner who has concerns about administrative tasks. Discussions of such topics as color of name badges, coffee service, and how to cancel a meeting gracefully make this book somewhat unique, although most of it is strictly nuts-and-bolts program administration.

Mead, M., and Byers, P. *The Small Conference: An Innovation in Communication.* Paris: Mouton, 1968.

Although Mead's chapters on the conference process are interesting and thought provoking, Byers' section on still photography as a method of conference analysis seems most appropriate for workshop planners. Documenting the stages of a program for later analysis seems a promising technique that might be useful in certain problem-solving workshops. The text and photographs provide a good illustration of this technique.

Murray, S. L. *How to Organize and Manage a Seminar.* Englewood Cliffs, N.J.: Prentice-Hall, 1983.

Referring to the seminar, workshop, clinic, or conference as forms of "instant education," the author proceeds to suggest what to do and when to do it. The usual administrative tasks of selecting a site, developing publicity, and registering participants, are covered. One unique feature of this book is the occasional "Ask a Pro" sections, in which the author poses a question to an experienced meeting planner and reports the answer. Readers may also be interested in the suggested contents of the "Handy Dandy Scout Box," a collection of "the everyday things you always seem to need [during a program] but never have with you" (p. 121).

Nadler, L., and Nadler, Z. *The Conference Book.* Houston: Gulf, 1977.

"This book is organized so that the various people concerned with conferences (that is, sponsors, coordinators, participants, suppliers, and so forth) would have some common reference points. It can enable them to recognize each other's responsibilities, though the focus of the book is on the role in which we have had most of our experience —

the coordinator" (p. vii). This book includes suggestions on the usual topics related to conference planning, but it also includes a chapter on linkage, evaluation, and follow-up that should have particular value for workshops in which transfer of learning to the work environment is especially important.

This, L. E. *The Small-Meeting Planner*. (2nd ed.) Houston: Gulf, 1979.
True to its billing, this book is concerned with the "dynamic forces" that come together whenever people assemble. Its strength lies in the chapters dealing with the effects of such design decisions as seating arrangement, type of audiovisual equipment used, and size of work groups on participant interaction. It also contains a well-written and practical chapter on evaluation.

Thomas J. Sork is assistant professor of adult education in the Department of Administrative, Adult, and Higher Education at the University of British Columbia.

Index

A

Altman, I., 21, 23
American University, video teleconference by, 81–82
Anderson, C. A., 69, 84
Audiotapes, as technological aid, 77
Authority and power, and learning transfer, 33–34

B

Bales, R., 21, 22, 23
Ball, S., 66
Ballachey, E., 23
Beckhard, R., 87–88, 89
Bell, A. G., 76
Benne, K. D., 7, 10, 22, 38, 89
Bennett, C., 56, 66
Bennis, W., 29, 38
Berelson, B., 74, 83
Bergevin, P., 4, 10
Blumberg, A., 21, 22, 23
Bradford, L. P., 21, 22, 89
Brethower, K. S., 79, 83
Budgeting, in planning model, 45–46
Bundy, C. E., 10, 84
Burke, W. W., 89
Buskey, J. H., 2, 40, 52, 69–84
Byers, P., 90

C

Cartwright, D., 20, 22
Cattell, R., 20, 22
Cervero, R. M., 1–2, 55–67
Change: defined, 28; refreezing stage of, 29–30; stages of, 26–30; unfreezing stage of, 26–28
Chin, R., 38
Clinic, distinguishing features of, 6
Coch, L., 17, 22
Cohesiveness, and effectiveness, 18–20
Collins, B., 15, 22
Commodities News Service (CNS), 82–83

Communication network, and effectiveness, 15–17
Computers: as technological aids, 78–79; in workshops, 82–83
Conducting workshop, and planning model, 51–52
Control Data Corporation, 78
Converse, P., 23
Cooper, S., 4, 10, 88
Course, short, distinguishing features of, 6
Critical Path Method (CPM), for planning, 41–42, 43–45, 51
Crutchfield, R., 23
Cummings, L. L., 38

D

Dale, E., 74, 83
Davis, L. N., 4, 10, 52, 53, 88
Demorest, C. K., 7, 10
Donaldson, L., 70, 79, 83
Doyle, M., 13–14, 16, 18, 22
Drain, R. H., 89–90

E

Etzioni, A., 31, 38
Evaluation: analysis of, 55–67; background on, 55; categories of, 57–65; of characteristics and outcomes, 64–65; of cognitive gains, 60–61; criteria for, 65–66; of design and implementation, 57–58; of learner satisfaction, 59–60; of learning transfer, 61–62; of participation, 58–59; rationale for, 56–57; resources for, 66; of second-order effects, 63–64

F

Facilitator, role of, 16
Farlow, H., 51, 53
Faust, W. F., 12, 22
Fisher, B. A., 12, 15, 16, 19, 22
Fouriezos, N., 17, 23

Fox, R. D., 1, 25–38, 62
French, L., 17, 22
French, R. L., 20, 23
Frye, R., 23

G

Gantt chart, 41
Garraway, H., 79, 83
Gibb, C., 13, 20, 23
Gibb, J. R., 22
Ginther, J. R., 74, 84
Glossbrenner, A., 79, 82, 84
Goals: conflict of, 32; defined, 31; and learning transfer, 31–32
Goldman, M., 14, 23
Goldstein, I. L., 78, 79, 84
Golembiewski, R., 21, 22, 23
Green, J. S., 61, 66
Gronlund, N. E., 61, 66
Grotelueschen, A. D., 56, 59, 63, 66
Groups: analysis of effectiveness of, 11–24; behavior patterns in, 15; categories of, by size, 13–14; cohesiveness of, 18–20; and communication, 15–17; composition of, and effectiveness, 14–15; conclusion on, 22; leadership of, 20–21; memory of, 16–17; motivation of, 17–18; and nature of problem, 11–12; process of, training in, 21–22; size of, and effectiveness, 12–14; task and maintenance functions in, 20–21
Guetzkow, H., 15, 22, 23

H

Hall, J., 15, 21, 23
Hare, A., 13, 15, 23
Harnisch, D. E., 59, 67
Harris, E. M., 1, 39–53
Harrison, R., 15, 23
Hart, L. B., 88
Haythorn, W., 15, 23
Heenan, C., 4, 10, 88
Heincke, C., 21, 23
Hickey, A. E., 79, 84
Hoffman, L. R., 15, 23
Hollingshead, A. B., 14–15, 23
Holmes, G. E., 10, 84
Hon, D., 17, 23
Hopson, B., 88–89
Houle, C. O., 56, 60, 67, 70, 71, 84
Huber, G. P., 38
Hutt, M., 23

I

Illinois, University of, and computer-assisted instruction, 78
Institute, distinguishing features of, 5–6

J

Jones, J. E., 22, 23

K

Kasworm, C. E., 69, 84
Kelley, D., 12, 23
Kenny, W. R., 59, 67
Kidder, L. H., 59, 61, 62, 67
Kirkpatrick, D. L., 56, 67
Klus, J. P., 42, 47, 53
Knowles, M. S., 6, 10, 70, 71, 74, 84
Knox, A. B., 56, 63–64, 67
Kochan, T. A., 31, 38
Kotler, P., 51, 53
Krech, D., 15, 18, 20, 23

L

Laird, D., 70, 71, 74, 77, 79, 84
Leadership, and effectiveness, 20–21
Learning aids: in planning model, 49; technological, 69–84
Learning design, in planning model, 48–49
Learning transfer: analysis of, 25–38; background on, 25; case examples for, 27–29, 31, 32, 34–35, 36; and change stages, 26–30; and contributing and supporting systems, 35–37; evaluation of, 61–62; and follow-up, 36–37; and individual performance, 25–29; obstacles to, 30–37; and role playing, 29, 35, 38; simulations for, 28–29, 32, 36, 37–38; and social organization, 32–35; summary on, 37–38; and values, 30–31
Leavitt, P., 15, 23
Lenz, E., 51, 53
Lewin, K., 26, 28, 29, 38, 52, 53
Lewis, R. J., 75–76, 78, 84
Likert, R., 20, 23
Linkage, for integrating change, 29
Lippitt, R., 89
Location, and planning model, 49–50
Longnion, L., 69

Lord, R. W., 90
Loughary, J. W., 88–89

M

McGrath, J., 21, 23
Maier, N., 14, 18, 19, 23
Marketing: factors in, 44–45; in planning, 44–45, 50–51
Mead, M., 89, 90
Michalak, D. F., 71, 84
Miles, M. B., 22, 23
Monson, M., 77, 84
Morgan, B., 4, 5, 10, 77, 78, 84
Morris, D., 10
Motivation, and effectiveness, 17–18
Mueller, M., 15, 23
Murray, S. L., 90

N

Nadler, L., 29, 36, 38, 53, 77, 84, 90–91
Nadler, Z., 29, 36, 38, 53, 90–91
National University Teleconferencing Network, 78, 81–82
Nebraska-Lincoln, University of, video teleconferencing by, 81–82
Needs assessment, in planning model, 46–47
Nevo, D., 56, 67
Newcomb, T., 20, 21, 23
Norms and rules, and learning transfer, 33

O

Oakley, N., 89–90
Oklahoma State University, teleconferencing network at, 78
Olgren, C. H., 77, 78, 79, 84
O'Sullivan, K., 69, 70, 77, 78, 79, 84

P

Pankowski, M. L., 1, 11–24
Parker, L. A., 77, 78, 79, 84
Participation, evaluation of, 58–59
Participation Benefits Scale (PBS), 59–60
Participation Reasons Scale (PRS), 59–60
Patton, M. C., 64, 65, 67
Pennington, F. C., 47, 53
Pfeffer, J., 33, 38
Pfeiffer, J. W., 22, 23
Planner: attitudes of, 52; role of, 40
Planning: analysis of, 39–53; assumptions in, 40–41; budgeting in, 45–46; and climate setting, 45; conclusion on, 52; and conducting workshop, 51–52; Critical Path Method for, 41–42, 43–45, 51; format related to time line in, 42–43; integrating time line and model for, 42–45; and learning aids, 49; and learning design, 48–49; and location, 49–50; and marketing, 44–45, 50–51; model for, 39–41; and needs assessment, 46–47; and resource person selection, 47–48; timetable for, 41–42; using model for, 45–52
Planning-Programming-Budgeting System (PPBS), 42
PLATO, 78
Power and authority, and learning transfer, 33–34
Problem: nature of, and effectiveness, 11–12; structure of, 12
Program Evaluation and Review Technique (PERT), 42
Projectors, as technological aids, 79

R

Rawls, D., 23
Rawls, J., 19, 23
Recorder, role of, 16–17
Resource person selection, in planning model, 47–48
Rewards, and learning transfer, 34

S

Sanctions, and learning transfer, 34
Sargent, S. S., 38
Satisfaction of learners, evaluation of, 59–60
Scannell, E. E., 70, 79, 83
Scheicher, J. G., 88
Seminar, distinguishing features of, 5
Shaw, M. E., 15, 18, 19, 23
Shenson, H. L., 89
Shipp, T., 46, 53
Slater, P., 21, 22
Smith, R. M., 10, 15, 23
Social organization, and learning transfer, 32–35
Sork, T. J., 1–10, 40, 52, 56, 85–91
Source, The, 82–83
Steiner, G. A., 74, 83
Stodgill, R., 20, 24
Strauss, D., 13–14, 16, 18, 22

Strother, G. B., 42, 47, 53
Suchman, E. A., 56, 67
Swingle, P. G., 38

T

Technologies: and abstraction continua, 74; analysis of, 69-84; applications of, 79-83; audio, 76-77; background on, 69-70; computers as, 78-79, 82-83; conclusion on, 83; defined, 30, 69-70; and interaction continua, and participation continue, 72-74; proficient use of, 71; and projectors, 79; selecting, 70; for simultaneous workshops, 80-81; specific, 75-79; telecommunications, 75-76; using, 71; video, 77-78; for video teleconference, 81-82
Telephone, as technological aid, 76-77
Thelen, H. A., 12, 24
Thibaut, P., 12, 23
This, L. E., 4, 5, 10, 91
Thorndike, R. L., 12, 24
Tuggler, F., 31, 38
Turner, R., 23
Tyler, R. W., 56, 61, 67

V

Values: defined, 30; and learning transfer, 30-31
Verner, C., 74, 84

Video, as technological aid, 77-78
Von Grundy, A. B., 12, 18, 24

W

Walsh, P. I., 61, 66
Williamson, R. C., 30, 38
Wilson, J. P., 49, 53
Wohlking, W., 78, 84
Work environments: and contributing and supporting systems, 35-37; integrating change into, 29-30; obstacles to transfer of learning in, 30-37; social organization of, 32-35; transfer of learning to, 25-38
Workshops: advantages of, 7; analysis of, 3-10; background on, 2-4; computers in, 82-83; defining, 4-5; effectiveness of, 11-24; evaluation of, 55-67; formats related to, 5-6; future issues concerning, 85-87; guidelines for selecting, 8-10; limitations of, 7-8; mission of, 39; planning of, 39-53; resources on, 87-91; simultaneous, 80-81; success of, 25; summary on, 10; technology in, 69-84; transfer of learning from, 25-38

Y

Yager, E. G., 71, 84

Z

Zander, A., 20, 22